THINKING ETHICS

THINKING
ETHICS

HOW ETHICAL VALUES AND
STANDARDS ARE CHANGING

Edited by
Beth Krasna

PROFILE BOOKS

First published in Great Britain in 2005 by
Profile Books Ltd
3A Exmouth House
Pine Street
London EC1R OJH
www.profilebooks.com

Typeset in Times by MacGuru Ltd
info@macguru.org.uk

Printed and bound in Great Britain by
Bell & Bain Ltd, Glasgow

A CIP catalogue record for this book is available from the British Library.

ISBN 1 86197 941 X

Contents

Acknowledgements

This book is the outcome of debates held in the five workshops of the 'Thinking Ethics' seminar, which took place in Geneva in February 2005. I would like to thank all the people who were so enthusiastic and supportive throughout, namely:

- the participants, who gave their time, experience and ideas;
- the people who could not attend but kindly referred colleagues who could;
- the individuals and organisations that provided the funds to make it happen;
- the journalists who agreed to write it up;
- the friends who believed it could be done and gave moral support;
- and, last but not least, all those who thought it was not a good idea, thus forcing me to improve the 'Thinking Ethics' project.

My thanks also go to Paul Forty, who managed the publication side of things for Profile Books, and the Philias Foundation, which partnered the seminar, and in particular Céline de Wurstemberger, whose organisational skills were invaluable.

Beth Krasna
Geneva, February 2005

Preface

'To be ethical is profitable, but to be ethical because it is profitable is not ethical.' And, one might add, it is also not profitable in the long run.

Peter Forstmoser, Chairman of the Board of Directors, Swiss Re, citing Peter Koestenbaum (*Heart of Business, Ethics, Power and Philosophy*, Saybrook Press, 1987)

Corporate Social Responsibility (CSR) has been part of my life for the last eight years. From the moment Laurence Fabry Lorenzini and I established the Philias Foundation, we knew that it would one day become Switzerland's leading organisation in the field of CSR.

However, despite this passionately held belief, we also met with many frustrations; the learning curve was steep and we had to do much hard work. Most of the companies and the consultants in this area tend to consider social responsibility as a part of business. This is absolutely fine, but they also think they have to demonstrate not only the societal but also the financial value of any input, carefully measuring the return on their investment in these activities.

Such assessments have certainly done some good in the field of CSR, encouraging a performance-based and professional approach. But is this all there is to it? Absolutely not! CSR should not need a financial or marketing motivation. It simply makes sense for the medium and long term to act responsibly, to be a good citizen of the world, in order to protect our planet from potential social and environmental catastrophes.

In this light, the 'Thinking Ethics' project has provided a wonderful way to meet people who are passionate about ethics in their field, and who don't consider life on Earth from the rather narrow perspective of finance or marketing, but are willing to look at the future in terms of what has to be done, or what must not be done.

Organising this event has been a great experience, and I would like to extend my gratitude to Beth Krasna, who gave the Philias Foundation the opportunity to participate in the making of what I believe to be a book of enormous relevance to our time.

Bettina Ferdman Guerrier
Founder, Philias Foundation

1

Introduction

Beth Krasna

Western societies have become increasingly participative and tend to disregard many forms of authority. Everybody wants to have a say. Users expect to be involved in the choice of norms and standards. Industrial and national standards organisations can no longer decide by themselves; use and markets will prevail. Even the geeks and technocrats who guard the Internet standards that allow such widespread and cheap communication are under attack. Some techies believe that the web sphere should reflect the diversities in society and that seamless communication can be maintained with translation technology. In many countries national committees have been formed to set the levels of use and research in genetic engineering; these committees are composed of people from various fields, such as politics, law, medicine, theology, academia etc. Often their proposals are subject to popular vote. Ethics, or behavioural standards, however, still seem to be debated in restricted groups or academic circles. Most people hear about the subject only when abuse cases are reported in the media. If we want to set behavioural standards in society, and if this can be done only with the agreement of a majority on the standards, then we need to get people to start talking about ethics now. We need to take over the discussion from religious and academic bodies and democratise the debate on ethics.

In order to increase public awareness of the issue and to seed the debate, the 'Thinking Ethics' seminar was launched in Geneva in February 2005. It was meant to be forward-looking, interdisciplinary and multicultural. Several specialists in various fields of ethics came together to brainstorm on five subjects: Ethics and Consciousness, Ethics and Knowledge, Ethics and Performance, Ethics and Disobedience, and Ethics in Real Time. They attempted to identify future scenarios and possible trends, and to discuss what will change, what might drive the changes and where the problems areas might arise in the next ten years.

As an example, take drugs that improve memory. Everyone agrees they should be used to help a patient come back to a normal level, as in the case of someone with Alzheimer's. But what about helping children perform better in school? Does the natural tendency to want one's child to succeed justify the distortion that would follow between those who have access to the drugs and those who don't? Where is the limit of free choice? These types of question were discussed in the Ethics and Consciousness workshop, which covered aspects such as the brain, psychiatry, relationships and awareness.

Ethics and Knowledge concentrated on the generation of knowledge and its transmission to society. The links between information, knowledge and wisdom were discussed, and the difference between 'knowing that' and 'knowing how'. Have we reached the limits of specialisation? Can science be ethical? Will ethics succumb, as the humanities have to a certain extent, to the quantification and measurement of scientific results? If we integrate science and ethics, will they contaminate each other?

A subject discussed in Ethics and Performance was sport. The use of performance-enhancing drugs in amateur sport is becoming widespread, but it is not controlled. In professional sporting events, despite the known prevalence of testing, some athletes still get caught using banned substances. What will happen ten years from now? Will the tests always be one drug late? Will genetic modifications be detected? Will the sports world declare that everyone should own his or her body and can consume whatever they wish, thus favouring the countries with the greatest means? These issues can be carried over to other fields: for example, finance, business and international organisations. Who will influence these trends? Public opinion, peer pressure, education or regulation?

When the subject of Ethics and Disobedience is raised, most people think of Gandhi or Au Sang Su Kyi. Today resistance to authority is becoming more and more violent. Will terrorism become an acceptable form of protest? In what situation can military personnel refuse to obey orders? Will we see more whistle-blowers and how will groups react to them, by protection or punishment?

In Ethics in Real Time the participants concentrated on cases where the time for response or decision does not allow for reference to an ethical framework, checking the facts or the protection of privacy. They also considered cases where there is a fine line between gathering news and gathering evidence. How will communication develop in a world which is more and more sceptical and where the message is shifting from 'trust me' to the public's response of 'prove it'?

Where did this seminar take us? A little further. Why should we care? Because everyone is concerned. It is our society, and we all need to talk about and decide how we want to behave in it. The results of the discussions in the workshops are developed in the following five chapters. These thought-provoking ideas are offered as the beginning of what will, we hope, be a widespread conversation. In parallel, you can follow or contribute to the debate at www.thinkingethics.org.

'Thinking Ethics' is an initiative launched by Beth Krasna, independent board member, in partnership with the Philias Foundation. Members of the steering committee are Eric Derobert, World Business Council for Sustainable Development; Bettina Ferdman Guerrier, Philias Foundation; André Hurst, Dean of the University of Geneva; Rolf Jenny, Global Committee on International Migration; William McComish, Dean of the Saint Pierre Cathedral, Geneva; and Angela de Wolff, Lombard Odier Darier Hentsch. The project was supported by the City of Geneva, Holcim, KPMG, Maus Frères, Syngenta, a private foundation in Geneva and several individuals.

2

Ethics and consciousness

Christine Wicker

- People do what gives them pleasure
- Ethical actions increase well-being, which is deeply pleasurable
- Helping people to connect helps them to be ethical
- Individuals who factor in all the roles they play – parent, spouse, consumer, employee, citizen – are more likely to behave ethically

Our brains are constantly being modified by experience and life events. So much so that the chairman of the Ethics and Consciousness workshop, neuroscientist Dr Pierre J. Magistretti, proclaimed, 'We never use the same brain twice.' This malleability of the human brain is called plasticity and lasts for as long as an individual is alive, which is good news for ethics in the year 2015. If old dogs do learn new tricks, the potential for change in ethical consciousness is far greater than many of us dared hope.

In the next ten years, humans will be asked to be even more open to the ideas and ethics of others. Excessive fear of such openness has led to an increase in fundamentalism, which is a danger to human rights all over the world. Our best hope for maintaining appropriate ethical boundaries and behaviour in a rapidly shifting environment is to empower individuals with a strong sense of their own identity and values and to provide them with a society that allows them to act ethically. The workshop concerned itself with how such individuals and societal norms might be strengthened.

As a first step, the Ethics and Consciousness workshop considered why humans behave as they do.

Human actions are directed by the conscious and unconscious mind. The unconscious mind is difficult to access. Psychoanalysis is one way. Religious exercises such as chanting or meditation may be another. Some believe such exercises can cause values to be implanted subconsciously. Others believe the power of myths, which speak to the unconscious mind in symbols that it recognises, can also reshape the unconscious.

The conscious and unconscious are being moulded by experiences within the environment, which means that society, whether represented by a group or the family or the larger social environment, can directly affect individuals at the conscious and unconscious levels through the mechanisms of brain plasticity. To say that our ethics can't be changed, strengthened and actually improved would be to fly against what we now know about the very nature of the brain itself.

Scientists who once thought that the brain stopped changing early in life now understand that every time we use our brain we alter it in physical ways that affect our capacities, our actions and even our perceptions. So, in a very real sense, we are what we do. We are also what happens to us. Each experience, whether pleasurable or painful, is reacted to by our body even before our mind has consciously grasped what's going on. Our body tenses or flinches or flushes with pleasure, and only then, after emotion has gripped us, does our brain begin to figure out what's happening. In other words, it is the body that picks fight or flight; the mind merely tells us why we're doing what we're doing as we're doing it. By the way it feels, the body tells the brain whether a given experience is good or bad, and the brain then draws its conclusions. These conclusions are carried over into the future as the brain directs the body to do certain things and to avoid others based on whether the body felt good or bad in similar past circumstances.

As a result, humans do what is pleasurable and avoid what is not, Dr Magistretti said. That rather basic principle is deeply encoded within the body and the brain. The first conclusion we might draw from that could be a dismal one for the future of ethics. If people never do anything that doesn't benefit them, they might rarely be ethical, because ethical behaviour often goes against immediate self-interest. But the human mind is a function of both the physical and the spiritual. Some people interpret this as meaning that a greater power or force has a hand in forming our personalities and aspirations. Others may use the term spiritual differently, but it seems clear that individuals please themselves by fulfilling desires of not only a lower but also a higher or more spiritual order. Sometimes they are happy to eat ice cream. Sometimes they are happy to avoid ice cream so as to stay slim. Sometimes they are happy to give their ice cream to someone else. All three types of pleasure – immediate, delayed and altruistic – can be employed to inspire ethical behaviour, although each one has its difficulties.

Luckily for the future of ethics, one of the most powerful feelings of pleasure that humans experience is that of physical well-being, which is often linked to an individual's embedded values. Acting in accordance with internalised values increases people's sense that they have a well-grounded, true identity, one that is separate from others and yet also part of a greater community of 'good' people. The human need for a strong sense of identity and the feeling of well-being this produces can hardly be overstated. Thus the biological connection between behaviour and pleasure might very well work to the benefit of ethics.

The fragmentation of people's identity brought on by modernity also has ethical dimensions. People often segment their lives, separating the various roles they play, so that, for instance, they think only as business people when at work, only as consumers who want the best value when shopping and only as shareholders who want high profits when looking at their portfolio. Such segmentation of identity can encourage people to behave without considering the overall impact of their actions. It also may cause them to feel a less integrated sense of their own identity, which can affect ethical behaviour. Therefore, members of our workshop reasoned, a person who takes all of his or her roles into account as decisions are made would be more likely to behave ethically.

The tenacity of the biological urge towards well-being

indicates that the future of ethics cannot be governed merely by laws or by the good intentions of any given group. It must rest on the consciousness and behaviour of individuals. At the same time, individuals who increase their sense of well-being by adhering to a set of internalised values might behave ethically in the face of all sorts of external difficulties.

Five specific areas of ethical concern for the year 2015 were addressed in the Ethics and Consciousness workshop: religion, business, the military, science and the media.

Religion

Religion will continue to be important in not only the next ten but the next fifty years, said Dr Christoph Stückelberger, Director of the Institute for Theology and Ethics of the Federation of Swiss Protestant Churches. 'If we try to put religion aside,' he said, 'it comes in the back door,' which is good news for the future of ethics, because religion plays a critical role in the formation of values. Values, in turn, are essential in the formation of individuality, and individuality must be maintained for ethics to flourish. If ethics do not have a place in the individual's consciousness, they are not likely to be active and successful anywhere else.

Four religious trends are likely to become more pronounced. The rise in fundamentalist tendencies, the increase in Pentecostal faiths and the growth of syncretism, which is the combination of various elements of different faiths, will continue. At the same time, organised religion will become smaller and formal religion weaker as informal religion grows stronger. Dr Stückelberger said that institutional religion ought to respond to new demands by being more transparent in its dealings, more open about its operations and, at the same time, more ready to engage with people of other faiths.

Respect for religious diversity and engagement with people of various faiths will be an essential ethic of the future. Bible classes that might once have been taught as part of a liberal arts education must be replaced with interfaith studies. This is not to say that the distinctiveness of each faith system ought to be compromised. The rigid attitudes of fundamentalists arise from insecurity, heightened by rapid changes in society, said Dr Stückelberger. To stem the increase in such ideas, individuals need a strong sense of their own values. 'The better rooted you are, the better you can deal with what happens,' he said. Dr Magistretti concurred by saying that the first step in pursuing ethical behaviour was to establish a firm identity within individuals. People who don't have a sense of themselves are less likely to behave ethically because they have no foundation from which to start.

This respect for diversity might not extend to fundamentalism, our committee seemed to agree, simply because fundamentalism so often fails to respect the human rights of others. The idea that fundamentalism threatened rather than furthered ethical behaviour seemed to be agreed upon.

Business

The workshop's three representatives of business came from multinational companies: Benedikt Vonnegut is Secretary of the Executive Committee of Holcim, Christian Kornevall is a Senior Group Vice-President and Head of Sustainability Affairs from ABB and Michael Stopford is Head of Global Public Affairs and Government Relations for Syngenta. All three companies have broadly defined responsibilities to stakeholders and the communities they work in.

Holcim Ltd is a global cement company with some 47,000 employees and operations in more than seventy countries. It has been a member of the World Business Council for Sustainable Development since 1999.

The ABB Group is a power and technology company with a commitment to developing alternative energy. It has more than 100,000 employees and operations in more than 100 countries.

Syngenta, a leading agribusiness company with 19,000 employees in more than ninety countries, has a publicly stated commitment to sustainable agriculture through innovative research and technology. It has committed itself to following the United Nations Universal Declaration of Human Rights in all the activities it has responsibility for.

Two examples of Syngenta's recent actions highlight how that commitment can play out. First, in May 2004 the company was accused of using child labour in India. After an internal investigation indicated that some children may have been used by contractors, the company hired the Fair Labor Association, a

US non-profit-making organisation that promotes international labour rights, to assess its India operation. Their report will be available to the public. Second, Syngenta has joined with Greenpeace and the World Bank in furthering a global analysis of world food needs that World Bank officials believe will make a decisive contribution to the reduction of poverty.

Each of these three companies works within many cultures amid various new demands for responsibility. These demands promise to intensify in the next ten years. The call for sustainability is something that concerns all the companies, now and for the future. Sustainability can be taken to mean that business ought to benefit the society around it rather than simply profiting from it. Issues of proper compensation, safety, health, taxation and civic participation might be involved. Sustainability is also used in an environmental context where it might address the depletion of natural resources or pollution.

A pressing concern for any company that hopes to stay in business is whether ethical behaviour pays off. As one member of the workshop put it, quoting the last line of an article in *The Economist*, 'The proper business of business is business. No apology required.' Healthy, profit-making businesses that can provide jobs, supply reliable goods and services, and pay taxes benefit society enormously. Some people argue that business is obligated to pursue those goals in all legally acceptable ways. Strengthening laws requiring ethical conduct would help level the playing field and clearly define what is and is not allowed, but ethics need to go beyond what the law allows. Making the argument that social responsibility is good for business and providing an environment where this is true will be increasingly important in the next ten years.

Our committee seemed to agree that ethical behaviour does strengthen a company in the long term, but in the short term it can weaken profitability. The stock market's demand for quarterly profits was pinpointed as a major problem. Hedge funds that prosper by quick trades in a fluctuating market work against the kind of long-term perspective that ethical business behaviour requires. Pension funds, which have a longer-term outlook, were suggested as a possible counterweight to the pressure for short-term profit. Members of the workshop also suggested that executive bonuses and other pay incentives might be tied to longer-term goals instead of being linked to the short-term rise and fall of profits. They expressed the hope that stake-holders other than company executives – citizens, shareholders, employees, consumers – might exert influence towards ethical, broad-range responsibility. Two important ethical questions they might address are: what is long-term success and how much is enough in terms of profit?

Benedikt Vonnegut noted that public ownership of companies also has a beneficial effect on ethical behaviour. Public companies have much greater transparency, he said, and are therefore more likely to answer for their actions. In addition, stock markets are becoming more transparent. The influence of publicly traded companies, with uniformly applicable global standards, can be an important factor in raising business ethics standards as global companies move into developing countries.

The increase in global business and the unique ethical problems it presents will only intensify in the next ten years. Christian Kornevall suggested that global companies ought to institute zero-tolerance policies for bribery in any form. His company was among sixty-two world business leaders in energy, construction, mining and engineering that signed a statement with the World Economic Forum's Partnering Against Corruption Initiative, declaring that they would have no tolerance for bribery and would implement or strengthen already-existing policies to make sure corruption was not present in their dealings. But Kornevall's concern with ethical boundaries went further than such obviously wrong practices. He also questioned whether companies are acting responsibly when they import consumer goods that are foreign to a culture's traditions. He asked, for instance, whether a coffee company should move into a tea-drinking country.

The increase in violence against companies and the ethical challenge of knowing what to do in the face of such violence are also pressing concerns for the future, he said. ABB lost six employees in Saudi Arabia in 2004 when militants were aided by insiders at the Saudi operation. As a result, all foreign employees on the project opted to leave the country. Should a company continue to endanger its employees in such circumstances? If it accedes to such pressure, will similar violence be encouraged?

Kornevall also talked about the impact of quick, cheap transportation that allows a product to pass through many countries in the production and packaging process before reaching consumers in yet another country. That practice can mean responsibility for the product is so diffuse that companies can more easily evade charges of unethical action. Globalisation can also present new temptations to companies when health problems at a particular site caused by pollution or bad practice need to be resolved. Instead of confronting such problems, a company might simply move away and ignore the situation.

Size itself can be a problem for rapidly expanding companies and for society, said Benedikt Vonnegut. From his experience at Holcim, he suggested that limiting groups to no more than 200 people can in itself encourage responsible decision-making. Top managers in large companies can interact with only a finite number of direct reports and subordinates. As a result, they can easily find themselves in an ivory tower – cut off from fluid, open communication. Limiting size helps maintain connections within and between levels. Delegating authority to local managers and encouraging dialogue across hierarchical levels can also foster individual responsibility and broader perspectives. Such techniques seem to encourage ethical practice in business, and they might work in society at large as well.

Vonnegut also said that the demand for global diversity might lead to more democratic companies. Fifty nations are represented among Holcim's top 1,000 employees, a configuration that automatically provides for considerable diversity of perspective.

Dr Stückelberger was optimistic about a strengthened role for non-governmental agencies. While their watchdog and advocacy activities will continue to be important, they might also be moving into another less adversarial role. He mentioned a recent effort among top coffee companies to cooperate on fair trade issues and said that a major stumbling block was that outsiders sometimes aren't willing to believe in the goodwill of corporations. In such cases, assurance groups could be included in the process. These groups, which might be non-profit-making, philanthropic or watchdog organisations, could monitor the agreements and vouch for the intentions of the companies. His coffee company example also highlighted the difficulties that can occur despite even the best of intentions. The companies were hampered by a reluctance to see coffee prices fall too low. They weren't concerned about their own profits, as cynics might expect; rather, they feared that if prices went too low, their suppliers would be forced out of business.

The military

In the next ten years, the protagonists in military conflict will continue to shift from army versus army to army versus terrorists and insurgents. Among the many new problems that this will bring is increasing difficulty in knowing who is and who isn't the enemy. At the same time, new weapons will allow soldiers to be further away from the damage their bombs inflict and thus less connected with the humans they are killing. Armies for hire are also likely to increase, and with them will come more questions about standards of conduct and punishment. Such a shift will result in a greater number of covert operations and 'secret' armies that are less visible to the press and the public.

The Internet may be a counterbalance here, as increasing numbers of people who are involved in conflict or have information about it post their information, opinions and ideas, which are then picked up by the established press. The International Criminal Court can also address illegality in military conduct but is hampered by the fact that not all countries belong to it. Among those that don't is the United States, which is also redefining norms of military conduct. The Bush administration's policy of pre-emptive war and its broad classifications of adversaries as unlawful combatants who aren't entitled to protection under the Geneva Convention are all new challenges to the ethical boundaries nations have set up.

To help preserve human rights in this world of shifting alliances and dangers, three steps might be taken, suggested Dieter Baumann, a lieutenant-colonel in the Swiss Army. Wars ought to be waged, first, only with a multinational force and, second, only with the permission of the United Nations Security Council. Third, every soldier ought to be trained to observe the basic human rights of adversaries. Language that dehumanises others ought to be avoided in military training, and the individual responsibility of each soldier for his or her behaviour should be reinforced. When some members of the workshop objected, saying that holding soldiers to such a standard might be asking too much, Lt.-Col. Baumann suggested that soldiers ought to think of themselves as policemen do.

'Police have to behave within the law, even if the criminals don't. It's the same with the army,' he said. Such a shift would also mean that soldiers would be willing to risk their lives not only for their comrades but to avoid so-called collateral damage to innocent people. As an example, he cited the decision over how high a bomber ought to fly. Pilots are safer when they fly higher, but the bombs they drop lose the pinpoint accuracy that would be possible if they flew lower. In such cases, the ethical decision would be for the pilot to put his own life at greater risk, said Lt.-Col. Baumann.

Science

The ethical questions confronting science promise to become more confusing in the next ten years. If we take one branch of science, neuroscience, which is the speciality of the Ethics and Consciousness chairman, Dr Magistretti, we get a good look at how complex matters are becoming. Brain imaging now allows scientists to visualise areas of the brain activated by emotions or decisions. As an example, when a person experiences romantic love or when moral judgements are made, two of the most private sentiments of human beings, scientists can see which areas of the brain are involved. Understanding the neurological basis of such deeply felt emotions and decisions may change our ethical framework by shifting our ideas about how much responsibility humans have for their decisions, which could have society-shaking effects on how humans view themselves, their religion and their laws. A lawyer might use neuroscience to show, for example, that a client's brain is wired differently from other people's and then argue that the client can't be held responsible for his actions in the way that other people are. Insurance companies might routinely monitor the brains of candidates for health insurance to rule out individuals with depression or other mental problems that might otherwise go unnoticed.

At the same time, new neuro-pharmacological developments might allow people to enhance their memory or alertness. Helping people with mild cognitive impairment, a relatively common condition that accompanies ageing, would seem to be a good use of such medicines, but what about using them on children or on people who just want an edge in a job interview or a test? These drugs have dangers as well. They affect synaptic plasticity, which is also a central determinate in individuality. One of the many questions that must be considered as these drugs become more common is whether they might erase the factors that make us who we are.

As scientists face a multitude of such perplexing questions in the next ten years, they can best begin answering them by remembering that they are not only scientists but also citizens and members of society. As the former, they may research for the sake of knowledge alone, but as the latter, they have a responsibility to consider the effects of their research on the community and to explain what they are doing to the community. Scientists, as any other individual in society, must not allow themselves to become like generals who are so far above the battlefield that they lose an emotional connection with reality and with the possible consequences of their decisions – or, for scientists, their discoveries. This emotional bond comes from being closely connected to other people in society and resisting the temptation to become isolated within the laboratory. Communicating the substance and effect of scientific advances is difficult and scientists may well resent the time lost from their research. 'But the public understanding of science is essential to the survival of science itself,' said Dr Magistretti.

The media

Various branches of the media currently seem to feed a worldwide addiction to bad news that is shaping the consciousness of humanity in negative ways. A steady diet of dismal, disastrous, mind-numbing events causes people to view the world cynically, to discount efforts towards improvement, to distrust others and to lose hope. In the next ten years, a move towards more balance in reporting would emphasise elements of hope and possibility that exist in even the direst of circumstances. Such a shift, which would rely on reporters individually looking for such stories, could have a major effect on world consciousness.

This is not to deny that the media have a responsibility to report on wars, threats, pathologies and corruption. Reporters are essential as a counterbalance to the positive spin that companies, governments and individuals put on their own activities. They are often viewed with disdain by the public because of their focus on bad news, but at the same time the public thirsts for an ever-increasing stream of such news. Once again, neuroscience may give us an inkling of why that is so. Current theories of emotions suggest that negative events have a much stronger effect on the body. People whose bodies are in a neutral state may feel little emotion, but when they read or hear a piece of news that shocks or angers them, their bodies react and suddenly they feel more alive. Too much bad news may sicken people, but nevertheless many will come back for more, just as though they were taking a drug that has good and bad effects. These 'bad-news hounds' are lesser versions of thrill seekers who pursue dangerous activities.

Our workshop referred to this as an addiction to bad news because it keeps people frozen in their current state of dysfunction, just as other addictions do. It causes them to feel helpless and to resist growth towards more healthy ways of functioning. The need for such news also seems to increase, crowding out positive images of the future that might break the habit.

This commitment to negative news is deeply embedded in journalistic culture and is unlikely to weaken in the next ten years. It is so strong, in fact, that working with think tanks and academics to change the focus probably won't yield many results. News executives, fighting for their jobs in the face of drastic market changes, are equally unlikely to lead the way towards such innovation. So, once more, individual consciousness seems to be the best hope.

Again, the Internet can act as a counterbalance here as people involved in news events are able to tell their own stories. Professional editors, who have functioned as gatekeepers for the news, are now being outflanked by Internet witnesses who report on their own stories. More and more often their stories are being picked up by the wider media. Just as these amateur reporters have broken scandals, so they will be able to balance and even challenge the negative stories of professional reporters. In the next ten years, they may also begin publishing stories of resilience and hope that will give the rest of us a more positive picture of the world we live in and our chances of improving it.

Individual reporters can be a powerful tool in changing consciousness once their own perceptions are broadened. Neville Hodgkinson, a former science editor with the *Sunday Times*, pointed to his own experience as a journalist. After years in the profession, he became more and more disillusioned with the narrowness of vision he identified in himself and his fellow reporters. A leave of absence allowed him the space to explore new ways of seeing his own consciousness and his place in the world. When he returned to his job, he began looking for different aspects within his stories that would highlight the aspirations and achievements of people as well as their failures or misdeeds. To that end, an organisation he works with now, Images and Voices of Hope, is supporting an international debate about the role of media as agents of world benefit.

To restate a major theme of the Ethics and Consciousness workshop: individual responsibility is critical in maintaining ethical standards. As Benedikt Vonnegut put it, 'Bestowing unconditional trust in our personal responsibility is the key.' He was speaking of his own company and its code of conduct, but his statement might have served as a motto for the workshop's conclusions as well. At the same time, the role of environment in allowing and even encouraging ethical behaviour cannot be overstated. Dr Stückelberger quoted St Paul in making a point about how often good intentions aren't enough. The Apostle said, 'For the good that I would, I do not; but the evil which I would not, that I do.' So a next step in thinking about ethics and consciousness was to look at ways that ethical behaviour is helped and hindered.

Dr Stückelberger focused on structural constraints that keep people from behaving as ethically as they might like to. The smaller the structural constraints, the greater the chance of successful action. He divided types of constraint into structures of nature and historical structures of human beings. Historical structures are political, economic and cultural. Some can be changed in the short term, while others can be modified only in the long term. Laws of the market economy would be long-term human constraints and shop opening hours would be an example of short-term constraints. Likewise, structures of nature might be those that can be changed by humans, such as genetically modified organisms, or they might be immutable laws of nature, such as gravity. When an ethical change is desired, it makes sense to concentrate on what can be changed rather than railing against what can't, and when trying to change long-term constraints great patience and time are advisable.

Connection

One of the most important determinants in ethical decision-making has to do with how connected individuals are with the results of their decisions and the people who will be affected. To illustrate, the neuroscientist Dr Magistretti recounted two stories of an ethical dilemma put to subjects in a study that was published in the magazine *Science*. 'A runaway trolley is headed for five people who will be killed if it proceeds on its present course. The only way to save them is to hit a switch that will turn the trolley onto an alternate set of tracks where it will kill one person instead of five. Ought you to turn the trolley in order to save five people instead of one?'

Most people said yes.

The subjects were then told: 'A trolley threatens to kill five people. You are standing next to a large stranger on a footbridge that spans the tracks, in between the oncoming trolley and the five people below. In this scenario, the only way to save the five people is to push this stranger off the bridge, onto the tracks below. He will die if you do this, but his body will stop the trolley from reaching the other five people.' Should you push the man?

Most people said no.

What is the difference? In both cases one person is sacrificed to save five, but hitting a button is more emotionally neutral than pushing a living person off a bridge. Brain imaging shows striking differences in the activation of brain areas involved. This might be interpreted to mean that emotional processing differs even at the physical level of the brain according to whether the action requires emotional, personal involvement or can be accomplished at a distance.

In the light of such understanding, it seems clear that ethical actions are more likely when people are intimately connected to the decisions they are making. Connection, then, would be a way for societies, groups and companies to achieve more ethical behaviour. Vonnegut's suggestion that organisations be limited in size is one way to achieve that goal. Hodgkinson's push for media to highlight hope-inspiring human stories of perseverance, success and transformation might also help.

There are many ways of disconnecting that allow unethical behaviour to proceed unchecked. Double standards are one. Denial and self-deception are others. Christian Kornevall talked about having been in villages where children were often sent away to work in the sex trade. Procurers would regularly visit the villages to describe the wonderful jobs that they could help the children secure. They would tell stories of how easily money could be made and how much better the children's lives would be. Parents could believe they were acting ethically when they sold their children. Underneath the lies told by the procurers and accepted by the parents, however, was a deeply hidden awareness that the children would not be coming back to their village and would never be heard from again. If anyone had told the truth, the system would have collapsed, but it was to everyone's advantage to continuing denying what they all knew. Similar situations occur in other environments. The courage to look clearly at what's going on – without excuses, denial or self-deception – is an important first step in bringing what's ethically right into individual and community consciousness.

Power is another way for people to disconnect from one another and from the effects of their decisions. The more people in power are brought into contact with those who implement their decisions and are affected by them, the more likely they are to feel responsible. To that end, people in power might periodically be placed in positions where they don't have the power they are accustomed to.

The environments we live in are also polluted with values that don't further the public good. This problem is likely to be even greater by the year 2015. The degradation of language, the glamorisation of violence and the trend towards consumerism affect the fabric of society in destructive ways. It was suggested that one solution was to remember that political fights are always about ethical matters. Once again workshop members pointed out that, when voting and speaking out on issues, citizens who consciously connect with each of the roles they play in society and act with all of them in mind are more likely to make ethical choices.

The discussion of Ethics and Consciousness began with definitions of consciousness and ended with definitions of ethics. What exactly was being talked about? Could we actually pin down a system of ethics that would work in a multicultural world? Did anyone have the right to make such judgements?

In a first stab at defining the ethics being sought, Michael Stopford suggested that the idea of tolerance and respect for others was a thread that seemed to run through the discussion. Tolerance must have some limit, however. Like freedom and justice, it can go too far and become a social ill rather than a good. Lt.-Col. Baumann interjected the idea that even during war respect for others' human rights is required, and ethical progress in the next ten years could see more attention being paid to the rights of combatants. He suggested again that respect for human rights ought to be included in military education. In addition, rules of engagement should stress the personhood of the enemy and require the use of non-lethal weapons whenever possible.

The most basic value is the right of an individual to live. To have food and water is a requirement of life, the most basic of human rights. Beyond that, protecting the right of a person to act as an individual and then to be free of constraints that keep him or her from acting ethically was posed as an important value if a society is to behave ethically.

The Universal Declaration of Human Rights, adopted by the United Nations General Assembly in 1948, was suggested as a good guideline for ethical standards that could apply across cultures in a rapidly changing world. The Declaration is a secular elaboration of the principles that all religions respect, suggested Stopford. Every faith has some formulation of the Golden Rule, which requires people to treat their neighbours as they would wish to be treated themselves.

The first ten articles of the Declaration were singled out in particular. They are as follows:

Article 1

All human beings are born free and equal in dignity and rights. They are endowed with reason and conscience and should act towards one another in a spirit of brotherhood.

Article 2

Everyone is entitled to all the rights and freedoms set forth in this Declaration, without distinction of any kind, such as race, colour, sex, language, religion, political or other opinion, national or social origin, property, birth or other status. Furthermore, no distinction shall be made on the basis of the political, jurisdictional or international status of the country or territory to which a person belongs, whether it be independent, trust, non-self-governing or under any other limitation of sovereignty.

Article 3

Everyone has the right to life, liberty and security of person.

Article 4
No one shall be held in slavery or servitude; slavery and the slave trade shall be prohibited in all their forms.

Article 5
No one shall be subjected to torture or to cruel, inhuman or degrading treatment or punishment.

Article 6
Everyone has the right to recognition everywhere as a person before the law.

Article 7
All are equal before the law and are entitled without any discrimination to equal protection of the law. All are entitled to equal protection against any discrimination in violation of this Declaration and against any incitement to such discrimination.

Article 8
Everyone has the right to an effective remedy by the competent national tribunals for acts violating the fundamental rights granted him by the constitution or by law.

Article 9
No one shall be subjected to arbitrary arrest, detention or exile.

Article 10
Everyone is entitled in full equality to a fair and public hearing by

an independent and impartial tribunal, in the determination of his rights and obligations and of any criminal charge against him.

To sum up, members of the Ethics and Consciousness workshop concluded that for ethical behaviour to have the robust nature it will need to face the challenges of the next ten years, the rights of society and the rights of the individual must be balanced. Too much individuality and too little are both dangers. It is the individual's personal consciousness that determines whether ethics will be maintained or abandoned. In the best of circumstances, people with well-grounded values and a well-developed sense of their own individuality would be supported by a society that shared and supported their values in concrete ways. But even when this is not the case, society and the future of ethics depend on each person deciding what is right and working to further that in personal as well as public ways.

Dr Magistretti gave a model for the type of individuality that the workshop hoped to further, quoting the words of Ralph Waldo Emerson: 'It is easy in the world to live after the world's opinion, it is easy in solitude to live after our own; but the great man is he who, in the midst of the crowd, keeps with perfect sweetness the independence of solitude.'

3

Ethics and knowledge

Tim Hindle

- There are increasing ethical implications as we progress from information, through knowledge to wisdom
- We need to bring ethics out of its ivory tower and into the real world, where it will be a major factor in decision-making
- There is a trend towards ending the fragmentation of knowledge, but we risk cross-contamination by integrating science and ethics
- Knowledge in general and science in particular must be used to find solutions to the major problems of humanity
- The main vehicles to bring about this reintegration are universities, schools, corporations and the media

Increasingly we say we live in a knowledge society and that we are all becoming knowledge workers. We no longer sell our brawn, as people did in the nineteenth century, but rather our brain. Our economic well-being depends ever more on our ability to find and use knowledge. And this is sure to continue. In the future we are bound to produce ever greater quantities of knowledge.

But does this require greater moral judgement? Do knowledge workers need to be more ethical than reapers and gleaners? Are the knowledge workers of the future compelled by the very nature of their raw material to make more ethical judgements than their grandfathers? In the past, manual labourers got up in the morning and headed to a factory or the fields, where they carried out their job, day in, day out. They did not need to spare much thought for the rights and wrongs of their actions.

Francis Waldvogel, the chairman of the group gathered to discuss the relationship between knowledge and ethics, drew a distinction between information, knowledge and wisdom. Information, he suggested, is the raw material for knowledge workers, much as seed is for agricultural workers and iron ore for steel-workers. Raw data, the stuff of scientific formulae and national economic statistics, is turned into knowledge by human intervention. There is no ethical dimension to pure scientific discovery, to Newton's laws of physics or to the fact that America's inflation rate is less than 1 per cent.

Pure science comes as close to reality as possible, to a reflection of the truth. As such it is value-free. When one passes to the subatomic world, Newton's laws are wrong; it is not a moral issue, merely the way in which science progresses.

William Davies made a distinction between truth and fact. It used to be a fact (a piece of information) that the sun went round the Earth. It was not, of course, the truth. Computers, he went on to point out, are good at providing information, but they are not good at providing knowledge. When the online bookseller Amazon tells you what books you might like to buy, it is not making a judgement based on knowledge but merely reshuffling data about your previous purchasing record. Governments and corporations make a mistake in thinking that by providing people with access to the Internet they are giving them knowledge. They are not. They are giving them access to a database (admittedly the largest ever devised) which people can, if they wish, turn into knowledge.

There are moral issues in the way that modern technology distances us from the consequences of our actions. Soldiers need only press buttons in a distant computer room for lethal ammunition to be sent on its way to destroy human life. In modern warfare, nobody sees the whites of their victims' eyes any more. Likewise those who create computer viruses in the solitude of their bedrooms and bring down IT systems that control heating and health-care facilities have no feeling for the victims of their actions.

Some worry that the uneven way in which information technology is disseminated (through the uneven ownership of computers and modems) is dividing society into a new variation of the old distinction between the haves and the have-nots. But the group felt that this is, if anything, a temporary phenomenon only. Nicholas Negroponte, a world-renowned IT expert from the Massachusetts Institute of Technology, said recently that he believes that a laptop costing as little as $100 will soon be on the market. He also maintains that it will soon be possible to distribute electronic hardware and software among groups of people so that each of them needs to buy only a bit of the whole system but things will be configured in such a way that all of them will be able to access the data of the whole system. This has the potential to reduce costs dramatically.

It was noted, however, that although we often talk as if everyone in the West has access to a computer and the Internet, the market penetration of these technologies still has a long way to go. In the United States just over sixty out of every 1,000 people own a PC; in Russia the corresponding figure is just over fifteen per 1,000. The mobile phone is a far more widespread product. More than 50 per cent of all Americans now own one.

William Davies made the point that wirelessness has latent redistributive properties. In many developing countries it has leapfrogged over the inadequacies of wired communications systems, giving the poorer inhabitants of many countries access to a powerful tool for wealth creation. In Turkey, for example, there are almost as many mobile phones per 1,000 people as there are in more developed countries in Western Europe, such as France and Germany. This rapid improvement in communications (which requires relatively little investment in infrastructure) has made a significant contribution to many countries' economic growth.

The group felt that there is an important distinction to be made between 'knowing that' and 'knowing how'. 'Knowing that' is being aware of information; 'knowing how' is having the ability to use that information. The Internet helps us to know that; it does not help us to know how. The difference is the same as that between understanding the contents of a car's manual and knowing how to drive a car.

In recent years stock-market analysts have changed from being a group of people who know that a particular company has this or that profit or turnover to being a group who know how well the company is going to do next year. The analyst has changed from being a person who was a mere messenger of data to someone who makes value judgements about the capacity of groups of people (the employees of corporations) to fulfil the expectations of others.

William Davies suggested that a main source of American dominance in the world is the extraordinary ability of its universities and other places of learning to turn 'knowing that' into 'knowing how'. Americans have a high capacity for mining raw data and turning it into valuable knowledge.

The purity of scientific knowledge

Both William Davies and Francis Gurry expressed some scepticism about the purity of science, as if it somehow exists in an ethical vacuum. Davies said that scientists are 'steeped in ethics as soon as they enter the lab'. Gurry felt that even the purest scientist has to exercise choice: for example, deciding from whom he will accept funding – governments, corporations or individuals. That choice inevitably involves a moral dimension.

Domènec Melé took the view that when a scientist prepares a set of experiments he or she has 'intention' to achieve certain goals and decides to use certain means to do so. To some extent, scientists can even foresee the consequences of their findings. All of this is part of the moral judgement of the planned experiments.

Since there is a person behind every experiment, ethics come into science from the very beginning. Not all goals or means used to gain knowledge are equally acceptable. The human dignity of every human being must always be respected. Melé was also keen to stress that the methods of natural science are not the only way of gaining knowledge. The social sciences and philosophy search for truth too, but in a different way, using a different methodology.

Jean-Louis Vanherweghem pointed out that scientific discovery is often serendipitous. James Watson was a physicist who, together with Francis Crick, stumbled on the double-helix shape of human DNA by accident. It is, Vanherweghem emphasised, very difficult as a scientist to start an experiment with an ethical point of view if you don't know what you are going to find.

Helen Sayers was keen to explore sources of knowledge other than science. What about the knowledge that comes from religion, art and culture, she asked? Not all knowledge comes from books and the Internet. Personal contact is an important way of transmitting knowledge and, even more so, wisdom. Once we have read things in books, teachers help us to understand them and enable us to know them.

The chairman then asked how art can have an ethical dimension. Helen Sayers said it comes from the intention of the work, the message that the artist intends to convey. Francis Gurry argued that art in itself does not have a moral dimension, although one may arise from the way in which it is received. Edvard Munch's painting *The Scream* may drive someone to suicide, but that does not mean the painting or the painter had an evil intention. Great artists see something that the rest of us do not and they move us by informing us of their vision.

Domènec Melé made a distinction between traditional art, which follows rules that allow the viewer to interpret the artist's message, and more modern art, which has few (if any) rules and invites its audience to experience the work purely on an emotional level. He recalled how many religious paintings and altarpieces have traditionally been used to transmit religious information, doctrinal contents or moral teachings, and to show role models.

Helen Sayers pointed out that knowledge also comes from experience; experience itself is a source of information, and that information can be turned into knowledge by the person who is undergoing the experience. She also emphasised that we need to value the power of intuition. This is, as it were, nature's guide to ethical decisions; it is a sort of common sense, and even children have it.

Francis Waldvogel wondered how we are to integrate these very different approaches to knowledge and ethics into our more traditional way of thinking about the issue. Francis Gurry felt he was not sure that we can understand them in the same way that we understand empirical scientific systems of knowledge. But, he argued, we should not lose sight of them, even if we do not fully integrate them into the system that we construct.

William Davies argued that there is an ethical dimension to the way in which people use the Internet. Internet sociologists suggest that it is an excellent technology for creating a large number of weak social ties, and that these have the potential to become a substitute for a smaller number of qualitatively more demanding ties of the kind that pre-Internet societies sought to establish. Davies suggested that these loose communities, constructed around the whims of increasingly narcissistic individuals, are at the core of the ethical issues raised by the creation of the information society.

The spectrum of knowledge

It is when the human mind makes use of raw data that the data begins to have a moral dimension. When the laws of atomic fusion are used to triturate Hiroshima and Nagasaki, then the amoral findings of science come to possess an ethical dimension. Information is transformed into knowledge by human intervention, when intellectual activity is brought to bear on raw data. When contextualised in this way, when related to a specific human need, only then do the discoveries of science give rise to moral dilemmas.

Jean-Louis Vanherweghem wanted to make a distinction between the transmission and the creation of knowledge. The creation of knowledge, he said, has an ethical dimension because all knowledge adds to the freedom of the individual. The transmission of knowledge also has an ethical dimension. For example, if I learn from the Internet how to commit the perfect crime and then choose not to commit it, I have made an ethical decision.

Domènec Melé asked whether ethics is about free choices or good choices. Vanherweghem said that without free choice there is no ethical decision. Not committing a crime simply because you don't know how to has no moral value.

Further along this spectrum – from raw data at one end to knowledge somewhere in the middle – lies wisdom. Helen Sayers wanted to make a distinction between knowing about a flower, all the facts about its botany and its science, and yet having no feeling for its beauty. This is having knowledge but not wisdom. Domènec Melé said that wisdom is 'the deep meaning of things', a higher level of understanding, beyond knowledge. Francis Gurry compared the difference between knowledge and wisdom to that between law and justice.

It is inevitable that a discussion of knowledge and ethics sooner or later gets around to Aristotle. Domènec Melé introduced the Aristotelian concept of *prudentia*, of practical wisdom, which in the ancient Greek philosopher's scheme of things was a virtue that can be acquired. To gain *prudentia* we have to search for the good in every decision, asking for advice from wise people and considering wisdom accumulated over the centuries.

William Davies referred to the philosophical distinction between knowledge, ethics and aesthetics. Knowledge is the pursuit of truth; ethics is the pursuit of goodness; and aesthetics is the pursuit of beauty. Where the ancient philosophers saw the three as forming a unity, the modern world is characterised by a split between the good, the true and the beautiful. We need to find ways of creating a better dialogue between those dealing in knowledge, those dealing in ethics and those dealing in aesthetics.

We have lost the beautiful fusion of the three, said Helen Sayers. Vested interest also often pulls them apart. In economic affairs, for instance, where too frequently we think only of how to maximise the size of our personal pot of wealth; and in art, where the ego all too frequently gets in the way and artists become interested only in their own fame. We should, she said, be asking how we can detach our selfish motives from our lives, how we can bring more altruism into our day-to-day existence.

'We all have an ethical sense,' said Domènec Melé. 'Speaking rigorously, there are no "economic actions", only "human actions" with an economic purpose. But these actions also have an ethical dimension, which should be considered. A deliberate and free action produces not only external but also internal outcomes. These internal outcomes include becoming more skilled and also transforming moral habits when the decision-maker realises that the action will contribute to meeting human needs in a fair way or will be detrimental to someone. In this way one becomes more just, generous etc., or, alternatively, is eroded in his or her humanity.'

Helen Sayers said that in parts of Africa there is an ancient word, *ubuntu*, which (roughly) means 'I exist because you exist'. Communities who understand this word come together before they make decisions that have an impact on the whole community. In Senegal a woman who was considering a proposal from Helen Sayers to introduce a course in values-based education brought together a committee of local representatives who discussed the issue for three hours. The agreement they reached at the end was one to which everyone was committed, one which everyone had, as it were, bought into. In the West such a decision would be made by a single leader who would 'tell' his or her subordinates what to do. While it may be quicker to take decisions that way, it is much less likely to be effective.

The ownership of knowledge

Francis Gurry raised the issue of patents and the protection of intellectual property, a controversial aspect of the commercial use of knowledge and information. The marked shift in the foundation of wealth creation from physical capital to intellectual capital over the past few decades has turned the spotlight on patents and other ways of protecting the rights to intellectual property.

Controversy at the moment is focused on three areas:

1   There is increasing conflict between the rights of the discoverers of new knowledge and other public-policy areas – for example, the firm whose research and development department, after years of expensive toil, discovers a new treatment for AIDS. How is it to price that treatment in the marketplace? There would be a huge demand for the company's product, but much of it would come from people too poor to afford anything like the price that the company could charge for the cure in, say, the United States. Yet in this day and age, differential pricing in different markets is scarcely possible. The Internet directs purchasers to the cheapest source of whatever they want to buy, wherever it may be. The lowest price becomes the only price.

2   There are growing tensions between long-term and short-term interests. The patent system protects the commercial use of knowledge for a fixed period of time. Some argue that this is too long to keep knowledge, which at the end of the day becomes a public good, out of the public domain. Inventors

say they have to go through such a prolonged series of tests these days before a new product can be sold that more and more of their patent time is eaten into by regulation. This sets those who see their mission as making knowledge available to the broadest possible audience – libraries, universities and scientists – against industry and those who are responding to the different disciplines of the market economy.

3   There is a broad feeling that the intellectual-property system is based too narrowly on a Western model in which the individual is invariably the generator of knowledge – 84 per cent of the world's patents, for instance, are owned in Europe, Japan and the United States. The biggest holders of patents are companies from America and Japan.

How is this system to take account of Chinese traditional medicine, for example, or African methods of healing? There is a growing feeling that it should provide proper protection for these different systems. One example given was that of a desert tribe in the Kalahari which for centuries has known that eating a particular cactus reduces the appetite. Western scientists latched on to the knowledge that the tribe had gained from long experience. They analysed the cactus and obtained a patent for a version of its ingredients that were duly recycled as a treatment for obesity. The Kalahari tribe obtains no benefit from this commercial use of their knowledge. It is a form of 'bio-piracy'.

Domènec Melé further considered the interplay of business and ethics. There are some, he pointed out, who believe that business should be an ethics-free zone: these are the people who maintain that business is business, and the rest of life is where emotions and morals come into play. He listed five areas of business where, apart from economic rationality, there is no escape from ethics:

1   Decision-making. In this essential part of all business activity, there is inevitably an ethical dimension when decisions may involve sacking people or promoting them, or deciding whether to buy supplies from countries such as Zimbabwe or Iran. Business decisions of this type cannot be ethically neutral.

2   Leadership. Business leaders today need to give moral guidance as much as anything. None of them can act as automata, relying on orders being blindly and unquestioningly obeyed. They have to persuade and cajole; they have to be diplomats and teachers.

3   Organisational structures and systems. This relates, for example, to the ways in which an employee's performance is appraised and rewarded, or people are promoted and moved around the organisation they work for.

4   The relationship between business and the society from which it obtains its mandate to operate. The idea of corporate social responsibility has gained much ground in recent years. Companies have been shifting from a mono-functional view of their purpose (namely, the maximisation of shareholder wealth and value) to a broader view of the moral responsibilities they have to a wider range of stakeholders – employees, suppliers and the communities in which the company works.

5   Corporate functions such as marketing, finance, etc. The

raising of money for new projects cannot be ethically neutral and nor can the selling of new products. Drug companies are regularly having to decide whether to invest in one potential cure or another. By deciding not to invest in one direction, they put at risk the chances of a specific group of patients ever finding a cure for their complaint. More and more drug companies are prepared to invest in potential cures only for diseases that afflict very large numbers of people. They see this as the sole way of finding the blockbuster product they are all looking for – the next Zantac or Viagra, for instance. The consequence is that if you have a complaint that only a few other people share, the chances of science finding you a cure these days are small.

Jean-Louis Vanherweghem said that although the pharmaceutical industry has produced many drugs that have benefited humanity enormously, it is an industry that is riddled with moral dilemmas. Concerns have been raised about the inappropriate pricing of drugs (which does not allow everyone to have access to treatment), and about the heavy promotion and marketing of drugs, such as Vioxx and other COX-2 inhibitors, which are known to have potentially damaging side-effects.

Research on human beings is also a moral minefield. For example, consider the case of a patient whose blood has been kept in a deep-freeze and years later is used to identify a gene. What right (if any) does the donor of the blood then have to the commercial development of this knowledge?

Further issues arise in the protection of privacy. There are obvious lines to be drawn between the distribution of knowledge for the public good and a patient's right to privacy concerning his or her own affairs. The human genome, for instance, is a sort of Internet of information about the human being. But how far can that information be used for the public benefit without it being an intrusion into the individual's right to privacy?

Only a few years ago, there were instances of people being tested for HIV and found to be positive, yet the person doing the test was not able to tell them that they had the virus. In the near future we are likely to carry passports which contain chips with information about our genetic make-up. Is this the sort of thing we want to be held in the data banks of dictatorial regimes around the world that we have had the misfortune to pass through?

The fragmentation of knowledge

A particularly significant feature of knowledge is the way in which it gets more and more fragmented over time. Renaissance man had an extraordinarily extensive pool of knowledge, and it was a deep pool too. Leonardo da Vinci could be at the forefront of several areas of science at the same time as being one of the greatest artists of his (and any other) time. Today, however, such people do not exist. We are all specialists.

As knowledge becomes more fragmented, so it becomes more unevenly distributed. Small groups of specialists are the sole gatekeepers of a particular store of knowledge. While 8,000 cardiologists are in New Orleans discussing the peculiarities of the emotive centre of the human body, 6,000 renologists may well be in old Orléans discussing the peculiarites of an organ all of three centimetres distant from the heart. But each knows little of the other's special interest. Would human health and well-being not be better served if these experts took a more holistic view of their subject?

Helen Sayers believes that there is a need for a holistic approach to education that brings ethics into every subject and that recognises the totality of the human being.

Knowledge workers are people who make decisions on whether to exclude or include information. They are the gatekeepers of the information society. Journalists' ethics are displayed as much by what they do not write as by what they do. Likewise doctors are as concerned about what not to tell their patients as by what to tell them. This growing group of people, the gatekeepers of knowledge, is sure to become increasingly important in our society.

The fragmentation of knowledge has been incredibly useful to humanity over the past 300–400 years, but its usefulness may be coming to an end. We are at a time when some sort of reintegration of ethics and knowledge is needed.

Francis Waldvogel compared the problem to the weaving of Oriental carpets (kilims). When the warp (the horizontal weave) has been completed it is not possible to see the pattern. Likewise when only the weft (the vertical weave) has been finished the carpet has no design. Only when the two are brought together does the full creation become apparent. Knowledge and ethics today stand like a warp and a weft that have not been put together.

We need to start weaving, because only then will the true pattern of human activity become apparent.

Francis Gurry suggested that one of the consequences of the fragmentation of knowledge is exclusion. People are excluded because there is unavoidably a host of specialities to which they are not privy. And exclusion is at the heart of conflict.

We all live and work in units that are too self-contained. The logic of the corporation does not work for the good of the economy as a whole; the logic of the nation state does not work for the good of the world as a whole. Systems have to be more integrated – we need more cooperation across borders, both national and corporate.

Ethics itself cannot be treated as one of these fragmented specialist subjects – as it has been in the past, set aside in an ivory tower and treated as a subset of philosophy. 'It has been put in a box – somewhere else,' said Francis Gurry. 'There has been an excess of secularisation.' Ethics has to be integrated into the teaching of all subjects, not just science and business.

Francis Waldvogel said that we would not be discussing this subject in this forum if we did not believe that teaching ethics from an old-fashioned ivory tower was passé. It needs to be brought out into the real world, into the world of decision-making and knowledge-generation. It is a basic element of human thinking, an inevitable part of the acquisition of knowledge.

Francis Gurry, however, warned of the potential dangers of such reintegration. 'We should be aware, after hundreds of years of separating religion, that the danger is of a return to fundamentalism.' We are ill-equipped institutionally to bring ethics back into a lay community.

There is a risk of cross-contamination – of science by ethics, and vice versa. 'We don't,' said Francis Waldvogel, 'want to go back to something that historically was self-contaminating – the contamination of science by religion.' That would take the development of mankind back several hundred years – to the days when everyone read the Bible as literal truth.

On the other hand, there is a risk that religion will be contaminated by science, which will impose an inappropriate urge upon us to measure ethical issues. We have already started trying to measure such things as social capital and trust, in order to fit them into our scientifically oriented epistemology.

Domènec Melé said that there are three ways in which such integration can be achieved: by force, by compromise or by harmonisation and prioritising. 'Ethics cannot be imposed in the name of science, and obviously ethics or religion cannot be a substitute for science. Nor does it seem a good solution to make compromises between ethics and science. This would be the case if one says that not everything in science is acceptable, but not every ethical requirement derived from human dignity is acceptable either. Ethics, like moral theology and religion, has its scope and science has it own. Science is autonomous from ethics in its methodology but ethics gives guidance to science to serve humanity. Thus the challenge is to find ways to harmonise ethics and science, but, where this is not possible, respect for human dignity should have priority.'

Attempting to quantify all the elements of social science may be dangerous. In a recent paper, Sumantra Ghoshal, a distinguished professor of business strategy, has pointed to one of those potential dangers. He argued that business-school graduates (MBAs) are being contaminated because their field of study has been overrun by modern economics and its excessive dependence on mathematical models. This, he says, has turned the study of business into a science, 'a kind of physics', and that, in turn, has freed business-school students 'from any sense of moral responsibility'. Hence scandals such as those that occurred at Enron, the corrupt Houston energy company where business-school graduates were as thick on the ground as hubris – and those that will occur at future Enrons too if the business schools do not change their ways.

William Davies pointed out that many of the recent corporate scandals in America came to light with the help of electronic media – through blogging and anonymous emails. Whistle-blowers these days have a powerful new tool available to them in the form of electronic messaging. Moreover, in several cases emails have provided crucial evidence in bringing corporate criminals to justice.

Domènec Melé said that the main problem lies in training the professors who teach business studies. Business schools, he believes, already have the tools for teaching ethics, but they do not necessarily use them. Many rely on what is called the 'case-study method of teaching'. In this, teachers work with written cases which illustrate particular business problems. Case studies are often put together without any particular ethical dimension. But that need not necessarily be so, although it is not easy to write about cases that highlight specific moral dilemmas. Many business schools, however, are trying hard these days to do just that.

On the other hand, there is evidence to suggest that it is not necessarily the business schools themselves that corrupt the students who go there. It may be that their very nature attracts people who are less ethical. Business-school students, for example, have been found to cheat more than students at other schools. And they have been found to give less to charitable causes than comparable students on other courses.

The reintegration of knowledge

Sir Francis Bacon said that knowledge is power, and the more knowledge there is the more power we have to do both good and evil. It has to be a fundamental principle of ethics today that the power of our knowledge be put to the service of humanity – in particular to solve the great issues of the coming decade.

In 2015 the three points of the global economic triad – North America, Europe and the Asian bloc – will still be the powerhouse of the world economy. The north–south divide will continue to be most apparent in Africa and diseases such as tuberculosis will still be with us.

A decade hence, the biggest problems that the planet will face will be access to clean water for all; the sustainability of our industrialisation; the urbanisation of our once rural societies; the spread of epidemics; and the level of literacy. It has to be the moral responsibility of science to address these issues and to attempt to find solutions.

Francis Waldvogel pointed to the way in which advances in medical science can sometimes themselves resolve ethical issues raised by the science. He mentioned, as an example, the experience with kidney dialysis machines. At first these were so expensive that they were rationed. But over time, and with more research, the machines became much simpler and cheaper to produce. Eventually many people who needed access to one could have it.

Before the Renaissance, science was not a top priority in the world. If science fails to resolve these five major issues facing us over the next ten years, then the pre-Renaissance state of affairs could soon return.

Helen Sayers said she thought that we have the tools to overcome the problems. However, we lack the ethical approach required to use these tools for the benefit of humanity. It is up to business, education and religion to call upon the greatest resource of all: human potential.

She also felt that we look too much into man-made systems. Science is only one of our knowledge systems; we need to tap into others. We all have it within us to do something great. If we accept that humanity is in a crisis, we have to ask ourselves, 'What can I do?' And a search for the answer to that question has to start with each one of us personally trying to live according to our own values, trying to be ethical individuals and inspiring role models. 'We underestimate the power of the human mind to use knowledge in an ethical way,' she said.

How can we integrate these different knowledge systems – of which science is perhaps merely the one we are most familiar with – in order to optimise our effort to solve these issues? What are to be the vehicles of this integration?

It was suggested that first of all we must look to universities and other educational institutions. Helen Sayers works with an organisation called Living Values Education, which uses a number of techniques and programmes to teach children around the world about values. It aims to provide educators with methods and resources for them to include values in all areas of their school curriculum. Its programme is currently being implemented in eighty different countries.

There is one question that such methods always give rise to: whose values are to be inculcated? Are they to be Christian values, Aristotelian values, Buddhist values or what? The organisation that Sayers works for has a list of twelve values which were found to be remarkably universal in a piece of research carried out by the Brahma Kumaris World Spiritual University. They are peace, respect, cooperation, happiness, honesty, humility, love, responsibility, simplicity, tolerance, freedom and unity. On one occasion when Sayers was training some educators in Burkina Faso to teach these values, a participant said, 'Oh yes, we have the same here in Burkina Faso, but we would not express them in your European way.'

In all efforts to teach these values to children, the teacher has to be a role model. He or she has to be a living demonstration of the values that are being taught. The educational process involved is one of proposing, not imposing, these universal values. It is also a matter of encouraging the processes of critical thinking in young people. In an age of information overload, it is ever more important to help people to make choices from among the welter of data that they come across. The skill of critical thinking, incidentally, is not necessarily linked to intelligence.

To demonstrate that the teaching of these values actually makes a difference, Helen Sayers gave the example of a school in Oxfordshire that decided to become a 'values school', using similar methods to those of Living Values Education. Within two years the school's academic standards had increased dramatically. The students were not just more ethical; they were also more successful in exams.

The group considered that we need to look also to the business and financial community to educate and to set an example. Large companies' budgets these days can easily exceed those of small countries. The GNP of Tanzania, for instance, is about $8 billion a year. There are literally hundreds of companies with an annual turnover in excess of $8 billion. The annual turnover of Exxon-Mobil, the world's largest company, is in the hundreds of billions. Its market capitalisation is over $380 billion and in 2004 the value of its shares grew by some 40 per cent – more than thirty times the value of the total output of Tanzania during the same period. In 1962, the British left-wing politician Tony Benn said that we should be sending ambassadors to the likes of IBM and Exxon-Mobil. If the idea had any validity then, it has ten times as much today.

Corporate rules of ethical behaviour must not exist just on a company's website; they must be integrated into the company's policy. It is, for example, unacceptable that companies sign up to various anti-corruption agreements (and mention the fact in their annual reports) and then establish subsidiaries abroad which they cynically deem not to be subject to the agreements.

Part of the problem is that there is no reward for ethical behaviour in the way that there is for knowledge or for information – and this is to some extent because there is no measure of ethical behaviour. The only reward comes in the form of reputation – a company's reputation for honesty, for example, will be rewarded by the business that comes to it as a consequence of that reputation.

William Davies mentioned the idea of the triple bottom line, whereby companies report not only their financial results but also their social and environmental bottom lines. This is a sort of attempt to measure ethical behaviour, but it comes up against the difficulty discussed earlier when science attempts to colonise ethics and reduce everything to a mathematical formula.

Jean-Louis Vanherweghem stressed that transparency is an important element in the transmission of knowledge and information. Without transparency we are not in a position to judge the moral value of the information that is being disseminated, especially where there may be conflicts of interest. That applies to business people as much as to scientists.

The group then addressed the complex network of nation states that we live with today, and the influence that it can have on inculcating moral values. Francis Gurry believes that the nation state has been shown to have enormous limitations. It is motivated to maximise one small group of individuals' particular interests. Yet it has pre-eminence in the international arena because the international machinery set up to deal with international problems is not working any more.

The United Nations system, in which essentially each country gets one vote, regardless of whether it is the United States or Burkina Faso, gives the United States (and other big nations) too little incentive to encourage power and decision-making to pass through the international machinery. The system holds together as it does largely because of the existence of the Security Council, which gives the world's richest countries a veto in key areas.

William Davies pointed out that we do not yet have a 'global public sphere' in which to air issues of global concern. Newspapers and other places for public debate are still largely national. The only type of media content that can currently be said to have anything like a global reach is CNN and Disney-style cartoons. Hopefully, however, that is going to change over time with the global dissemination of digital technology and further penetration of the Internet.

Once we do have a global public sphere, though, who is going to be its gatekeeper, the arbiter of what should appear in it?

The group agreed that we are desperately in need of a new system of international cooperation, one that will involve less power for nation states and include more cross-national activity. States are power structures that are built to survive. The more powerful they are and the longer they have been around, the less likely they are to delegate responsibility to international or cooperative cross-border organisations.

But technology's indifference to borders has changed the

international dimension of issues today. For example, the growth of pan-Arab media in general, and of the television station Al-Jazeera in particular, has made the whole Arab world aware of democratic changes in Afghanistan, Iraq and Lebanon. Seeing what is possible in neighbouring countries has made others wish for the same. Yet never has the status of the international machinery for addressing such cross-border issues been so low.

Francis Gurry believes that individuals must develop a tran-scendental philosophy, one that reaches beyond the company they work for and the nation that gave them a passport. People need to think of themselves as citizens of the world; only then will they realise the futility of trying to stop germs at a border crossing.

It would help if there were four or five examples of transcen-dental organisations that are setting out to solve the great global problems of the coming decade. The Global Fund to Fight Aids, Tuberculosis and Malaria is one of the few examples of an organi-sation that is trying to escape from the traditional model. Half of its board consists of representatives of private-sector donors and half of public-sector donors. So far the fund has pledged to give $3 billion to organisations in 128 different countries.

Ideally, such organisations need to be project-based, tackling issues one by one. And they need to be fluid, so that they can appear in different shapes and sizes to suit the issue at hand.

William Davies wondered why the threatened environmental disaster of global warming has not yet pushed us towards recog-nising this need for universal identity. Nations' identities, he suggested, are forged by battles and threats; yet the threat of global warming has not had the binding effect that might have been expected. Helen Sayers wondered if that was correct. Disasters, she said, do bring us together: the tsunami in South-East Asia elicited extraordinary universal sympathy, as did the attack on the World Trade Center on 11 September 2001.

It was agreed that the media have a key role to play in the process of reintegration and education. They are one of the key gatekeepers that decide what information is turned into knowledge – creating 'stories' with an ethical dimension from 'facts' without one. Universities and other educational institutions also play the role of gatekeeper, deciding what information young minds have access to and the ways in which that information is presented to them.

Jean-Louis Vanherweghem said that it is important to give these gatekeepers freedom, but at the same time they must declare when and where there are conflicts of interest. In universities, for instance, there is often a conflict between the economic interest of the institution and its academic freedom. On occasions, subjects are encouraged because there are sponsors prepared to fund them.

Likewise the media can be compromised in several ways – by the political or commercial interests of its owner, for instance, or by the economic interest of the individual bearer of the message, the journalist or presenter.

How can economic interests be fitted into all this? How can business obtain knowledge and make a profit out of it in an ethical way? Domènec Melé said that in the first instance companies should set out their values in a mission statement. But this must be more than a set of rules pasted into their website. Many companies have a conflict between their management objectives and the goals of their mission statement. They need to think carefully what it means to implement the rules of that statement. Every frontline manager has to sign up to his or her company's ethical standards. By and large, people are more satisfied in their lives if they feel that what they are doing is admirable, good and ethically responsible.

4

Ethics and performance

Garrick Holmes

- Today performance is
  - mainly economic/financial and short-term in the private sector
  - judged on how well it serves the public good in the public sector
- Ten years from now there will be
  - a more balanced approach, including social and environmental as well as financial considerations, in the private sector
  - a more rigorous cost/benefit evaluation of public performance
  - a proliferation of ratings and standards that incorporate social and environmental criteria, giving more transparency
  - an increase in importance of managing reputations
- The driving forces of change include globalisation, money, regulation and other forms of ethical control, with 'chaos' as an agent of change
- The players will be businesses, shareholders, institutions, the media, NGOs, the government, consumers and academics

Our discussion group had backgrounds in a variety of professions – finance, auditing, science, sport and an NGO (non-governmental organisation) focusing on corruption. Each has its own set of issues that are ethical and performance-oriented. We looked at what are the key factors in ethics and performance, how the relationship between the two might change over the next ten years, the drivers of that change and who will lead it.

Ethics is a hard thing to define or quantify. It has to do with conduct that meets approved standards. Ethics is abstract, but becomes real in specific cases. For instance, a drug that plays a life-saving role in kidney dialysis has also been used to enhance the performance of Olympic athletes. Ethical issues and tensions have always existed, but many more people today are being drawn into the discussion.

Performance has to do with the quality or results of human activity, whether individual or collective. The problem is how to combine ethics with performance, so that performance incorporates ethical considerations in a practically applied framework.

Key factors

Long-term vs. short-term
The group endorsed an idea expounded by Heidi Diggelmann, a Swiss medical scientist, that ethical performance entails long-term thinking. 'In whatever you do,' she said, 'you must think about the long-term effects for global society. Because if you look at the short-term level for a small sector of society, some issues

may appear obviously performance-positive. It's only when you start looking at long-term effects and take into account the well-being of society – and of all life on this globe – that the question arises of how many risks you are going to take for how much potential benefit. In ten years' time I would hope we will all have started thinking about activities in a very long-term perspective – at least a generation or maybe two.'

Others agreed that it is essential to take a long-term perspective – but very difficult, because everyone is measured, individually or collectively, on a short-term horizon. Politicians are re-elected or not on the basis of four or five years' performance, the performance of employees is reviewed each year, companies are measured by the market on their quarterly performance.

But if a given performance looks poor or unprofitable in the short term, in the longer term this might change. What can also alter with the passage of time is an apparent contradiction between your own personal interests and the broader societal or global interest. As Raphael Jaquet, the head of auditing firm KPMG's Geneva office, pointed out, 'Early investors in China lost a lot of money at first, but in the long run it was good for them as well as for the Chinese. Today they may be well positioned because they made that investment. So short-term bad can be long-term very good.'

Financial vs. non-financial criteria
Traditional definitions of performance in the private sector are mainly economic/financial and short-term. Ethical performance – moving towards an ethical goal – involves value creation, which

leaves room for non-economic criteria. 'Many people think a good economic performance is not achievable with ethical criteria,' said Dominique Biedermann, Executive Director of Ethos Swiss Investment Foundation for Sustainable Development. 'I disagree. Value creation is not only financial/economic, but also of other values, such as solidarity, peace or freedom.'

In fact, non-financial criteria also commonly figure in business. 'When we evaluate our people at KPMG,' explained Mr Jaquet, 'we have quantitative and qualitative performance measures. Without the financial, you fail. But you need both. Performance is the point of equilibrium between long-term investment and short-term reward.'

Robin Hodess, Director of Policy and Research at NGO Transparency International, summed up this point as follows: 'Performance is the value added by behaviour. Performance is about value creation – it may be profit-oriented, but also creating values. In ten years we want to move towards ethical performance.'

Public vs. private sector

Ethics and performance differ between the private and public sectors. As Ms Hodess put it, 'Governments are given a much longer leash to make mistakes; they waste a lot of money. In the private sector the bottom line counts, so they are punished more quickly. The public sector isn't evaluated by its financial performance. They are given budgets and they have to spend them. It's a question of how accountable they are, what they achieve from that spending, what the results are. Their assignment is by nature to provide some public good.'

Nevertheless, she added, measurement and assessment of performance are also increasing in the public sector, 'largely because of the huge gulf between what they've achieved and the money they are spending on it'. If financial criteria have been underemphasised in the past, the public sector now faces pressure from taxpayers to provide value for money. As Dr Diggelmann noted, the academic world too is increasingly being held account-able to prove its contribution to society.

She also mentioned one instance of the double standard of ethics between public and private that is difficult to rationalise. In certain countries, notably the United States, human embryonic stem cell research is encouraged in the private sector but forbidden in the public.

Another aspect of the private/public double standard concerns personnel policies. In the public sector, said Dr Diggelmann, 'You don't have same freedom to hire and fire the best and worst people.' Mr Biedermann argued, 'There is a social performance in the public sector – employing people is value-creating. Even if they work slowly, it is better to keep them off the streets.'

One way of bridging this gap, suggested Mr Biedermann, would be to inject social/environmental criteria into public-sector tendering – the number of apprentices, say, or the percentage of disabled workers employed by a bidder could be taken into consideration, although price would remain the main factor. A recent ruling by the European Court of Justice allows environ-mental considerations to be taken into account.

Competing roles and mainstreaming

Another issue raised by Mr Biedermann is the coherence between the different roles we play. 'Everyone is playing several roles, as a consumer, a parent, a career person, a shareholder (direct or through their pension fund), a member of civil society. The challenge is to make our ethics and our performance metrics coherent across all these roles.'

Dr Diggelmann offered an answer: 'Ethics was formerly a subject that was taught separately, with its own specialists. But what we need is ethics to become part of all our activities, to become an integral part of how you do your thing, in private or public, as a citizen, consumer – a sort of ethics mainstreaming.'

Individual vs. collective

Matt Christensen, Executive Director of the European Social Investment Forum (Eurosif) and chairman of our session, observed that there is often a tension between our own individual performance and that of our company or organisation. This leads to difficulties in trying to make the whole unit work together cohesively, as opposed to pieces of it.

'Box-ticking' vs. core values

'You can't necessarily inculcate ethics,' said Mr Christensen. 'Even if you try to create the best guidelines in the world, they can very easily become a "box-ticking" exercise that doesn't necessarily change the nature of performance. Box-ticking is not enough – you need to create values that are core and bring these into the organisation (and not just for PR purposes).'

Mr Jaquet of KPMG concurred: 'In auditing, we see more and more over-regulation – it is misleading, it gives the illusion of propriety, that you are doing things right because you obey the rules. And too many rules become a burden.'

Universal vs. relativism

Globalisation raises the question of whether ethical standards are universal or relative – for example, in differing attitudes towards bribery and corruption. Are ethics and performance relative, for example, between north and south? Is there a way to create common threads? How can we come up with shared ethical principles and performance metrics?

Participants were divided on this issue. Some stressed that there are certain ethical norms of universal application, others that there are different understandings of what is ethical performance.

'There is a capacity in all societies to draw the line somewhere between right and wrong,' Ms Hodess maintained. 'Cultural relativism is a slippery slope.' Pâquerette Girard Zappelli from the International Olympic Committee agreed: 'Despite cultural and religious differences, some things are considered unethical by everyone everywhere – there are some agreed ethical norms. Bribery and corruption are unacceptable everywhere. In a globalised society, we have to try to find a medium level – not too high, but not too low.'

Others leaned towards the relativist view. 'For us, value-creation means something else than for people from poor countries,' said Mr Biedermann. 'For us, things are going pretty well, but we're trying to fix at the margins, maintain quality standards and so on, as opposed to getting on the first rung of the ladder. The perspectives are very different.'

'It depends not only on culture but on standards of living,' said Ms Girard Zappelli. 'For example, in some countries putting children out to work is the only way to feed the family. Over time, more prosperity and rising living standards will raise the level of affordable ethics.' Admittedly, this optimistic scenario is hostage to unforeseen setbacks, like AIDS in Africa or the ten-year drop in longevity of Russians since the collapse of the Soviet Union.

Mr Christensen added, 'Some circumstances force conduct that is recognised as unethical – for example, Thai parents selling their daughters into prostitution even though they know it is wrong. Otherwise their basic needs would not be met.'

How to bridge the ethical gap? Dr Diggelmann described her experience in a major north–south research project. 'In practice,' she concluded, 'equal dialogue between the partners, defining common ethical goals together from the start, is the key to reaching those goals in the long term.'

In her paper for the workshop, describing the work of Transparency International against corruption, Robin Hodess sounded a similar note: 'We do not have a heavy-handed, top-down approach to building our network around the world. Instead, we have set up alliances based on mutual trust and clear responsibilities from both sides, backed up by an accreditation procedure that takes stock of this relationship – and is mindful that the reputation of our organisation worldwide depends on the accountability of its affiliates.'

Horizon 2015

Peering into the future, participants saw some significant changes emerging within the next ten years. Among these are changes in the definition of ethical performance and how it is evaluated; a growing 'reputational risk' for businesses that do not measure up; and possibly an awakening of the general public to a new sense of ethical responsibility – although ten years may be too short a period for such a fundamental change.

Performance = value creation
The definition of performance is already changing, in both private and public sectors. For businesses, where there has been too much emphasis on financial criteria, in the future there will be a more balanced approach including financial, social and environmental considerations – the 'triple bottom line' of the CSR movement. Public institutions, where there has been too little accountability, will be subjected to a more rigorous cost/benefit evaluation of their performance. Although civil servants will resist such monitoring, the trend is already apparent, and in ten years some sort of performance measures and incentives will be in place.

Ms Hodess summed it up: 'In business, you will have these other bottom lines. In other organisations, there will be more vigilance in how they are serving the public good.'

Evaluation
With changing definitions, the valuation of performance will also change. In the private sector, there will be a proliferation of

diverse ratings and standards that incorporate social and environmental criteria, which will confuse people while at the same time galvanising action. As Mr Christensen said, 'Companies will be confused over how many to answer, who is behind them, how important it is to respond. There may be some harmonisation over time, but meanwhile there will be some noise and confusion. These standards and ratings are going to start slowly to influence the shape of the system, and ten years from now we may see a significant change in some of the ways things are done.'

'We need measurement and rankings, because otherwise people are unaware,' said Beth Krasna, the organiser of the seminar. 'In the next ten years we're going to see all kinds of players coming up with their own ranking systems on the criteria that they're interested in. We are seeing this in universities now. And companies will look to see how they are ranked. To improve their reputation, they may decide to modify their performance. It could be superficial at first, but something stays in the values.'

All this will mean greater transparency, leading to greater awareness on the part of the public. 'Awareness is crucial,' said Mr Jaquet. 'Transparency leads to awareness. The three pillars of performance are financial, social and environmental. In ten years company reports will have much more on the latter two, and more transparency.'

Mr Biedermann suggested that performance assessments will be based more on the future than on the past – in corporate efforts to manage the risk of climate change, for example. 'Today, people are asking companies how they performed in the past, and how they expect sales and profits to grow in the future. In the future, you will be pressed to look forward on non-financial goals as well – job creation, environmental problems like Kyoto. What are your objectives for the future, so next year we can measure if you have reached your goals? And if not, what corrective actions you are taking?'

To some extent this forward-looking orientation reflects the changing nature of ethical problems, particularly those relating to the environment. As Mr Christensen pointed out, 'Climate change poses the risk that the warnings won't be big enough to alter our behaviour, and when something major finally happens it will be too late.'

In a paper submitted to the conference, Mr Jaquet quoted the French writer Antoine de Saint-Exupéry: 'We do not inherit the Earth from our parents, we borrow it from our children.'

'How do we change the balance in favour of Kyoto compliance?' asked Mr Jaquet. 'We need sanctions or incentives to force companies to make the necessary investments.' Thanks to the EU's new emissions trading scheme, in fact, companies that succeed in cutting their emissions of greenhouse gases will reap a financial reward by selling their unused emission allowances to others who have been less successful.

Reputational risk
A more general form of sanction or incentive for ethical performance is the risk or reward to a company's reputation. This equation is changing quickly, with the growth of CSR and new accounting rules requiring much more information on the non-financial performance of companies in their annual report.

'Companies put a high value on their image,' explained Mr Jaquet, citing the classic case of Nestlé and powdered milk in Africa. 'Reputation, also known as branding, is a driver for companies to maintain or increase their value, because they gain a competitive advantage, and there is a threat of exposure to sanctions if they do not behave properly. This is taken very seriously. If your branding is good, you will attract better people. And with better people, you might make more money.' Hence the attraction of CSR.

The cost of managing reputation will rise, warned Ms Krasna. Organisations will have to comply with regulatory bodies but also respond to NGOs and other reputation or image agents. And to deal with reputational risk, they will need to invest in 're-educating' their people, providing ethics sensitivity training either internally or through courses offered by professional or academic institutions. 'Reputational risk will increase in ten years. Not just the media but individual groups will have their voices heard, because the technology exists now. And maybe within the organisation, if they are measured, people will start wanting change from within. But you can have a reputational problem anywhere in the company as decisions are delocalised within it. Somebody fairly down the line can make a decision that can create a huge reputational risk for the organisation. So if you want to ensure that the people collectively adhere to the values of the company, so that you don't have these problems in the future, then you have to make sure they know what the values are, that they have the education, the training that they need.' She cited the example of Citigroup, which after a series of scandals has announced mandatory training on ethics for all employees.

Best practice and peer pressure

'Where Citigroup leads, all the other banks will follow,' predicted Mr Jaquet. Indeed, organisations that set an example of best practice will not only enhance their own reputation but leverage peer pressure on others that constitutes an important form of sanctions.

'In many ways misbehaviour has social sanctions,' said Dr Diggelmann. 'Behaving correctly in every society or group is often because of peer pressure, even without legislation or ethical guidelines. You exercise self-control because you want to be part of the group.'

Awakening the public?

Some participants suggested that in ten years we will see an awakening of the general public to a feeling of responsibility for ethical issues. 'Who awakens civil society?' asked Ms Girard Zappelli. 'Part of the work is done by NGOs. Also the media have to transmit information.'

'If we're relying on society to change, on increased public engagement and a new activism, ten years is too short,' cautioned Ms Hodess. 'But one change I am confident of is that there will be more emphasis on ethics ten years from now – a mainstreaming of ethical considerations.'

Change drivers

In the course of our discussions, a number of driving forces of change were identified. In addition to reputational risk, as discussed above, these include globalisation, money, regulation and other forms of ethical control, with 'chaos' as an agent of change.

Globalisation

'People's knowledge of what's happening in the world is much greater today,' said Ms Hodess. 'Take the speed and depth of the public response to the Asian tsunami. The media coverage means these things are present in our lives. With the economy rapidly globalising, there is felt to be a need to develop the other dimension, the human side. Businesses are internationalising; money flows; the role of international financial institutions, particularly in the south, is enormous.'

Regulation

An obvious driver of change is new regulation. But while this is often inspired by ethical reflection, it is not necessarily the most effective guarantee of ethical performance. 'Some laws go too far – and crooks will always circumvent them,' Ms Hodess pointed out, adding, 'Many corrupt countries have good law.'

There is also the danger of 'box-ticking' already mentioned. Ms Girard Zappelli, a former judge, quoted a French adage, *Trop de loi tue la loi* (Too much law kills the law). 'When it's too much, we miss the need to decide in our own minds on personal guidelines. Too much regulation stops people from deciding what is the right thing to do and taking responsibility, deciding for themselves what is ethical performance or not. And no legal system can prevent wrongdoing.'

Nevertheless, she added that in certain cases regulation can have an ethical impact – for example, a French law requiring minority quotas for disabled workers. But for Mr Christensen, 'This raises the problem of positive discrimination. When does it become bad?'

An alternative approach is 'soft law', such as voluntary codes, guidelines put forward by professional institutions, or the recent recommendations from the European Commission on corporate governance. Such guidelines and recommendations, although not legally binding, can enforce ethical standards through peer pressure and the media. In some cases they are eventually translated into legal obligations.

In her paper for the workshop, Heidi Diggelmann stressed the important role played by self-regulation through voluntary professional guidelines for scientists. 'In scientific research, the commitment to truthfulness is indispensable. It is the basis of all scientific activity. It is also a precondition for the credibility of science and the foundation for the privilege of freedom of scientific research. As adherence to these standards can scarcely be assured by the law or by the state judiciary, primarily science itself has to provide its own regulations in this respect. Procedures for how to act in cases of alleged misconduct must be established.' Thus the Swiss Academy of Medical Sciences, of which she is an honorary member, has drawn up a set of guidelines for scientific integrity in medical and biomedical research.

Finally, there is the sanction of the market. 'Where there is market pressure,' said Mr Jaquet, 'you don't need law to bring about change.' On the other hand, Dr Diggelmann noted,

'Sometimes ethical things are not being done because there is not enough market pressure – for instance, the development of vaccines for malaria.'

Money

While money is the traditional driver of performance, it is only one of the drivers of the move towards ethical performance, and not necessarily the most potent.

Sometimes the incentive can be indirect – the hope of 'doing well by doing good'. As Mr Jaquet put it, 'In the competitive arena, if you create value around the image of a company, if you are perceived by the global market as one of the players who is concerned by long-term investment value, you will benefit in the short term because you are the one who is chosen by the client because you are differentiated from the others. It's a win-win situation.'

A more direct connection between money and ethical performance is the socially responsible investment (SRI) movement, which looks for business opportunities that also have a social or environmental bonus. So far this is a marginal approach, currently representing only about 1 per cent of financial market capitalisations – but that is up from 0.001 per cent ten years ago. In another ten years, speculates Mr Christensen, who leads a European forum on the subject, the figure might go to 10 per cent. In his paper for the workshop, he asserted that taking into account non-financial performance does not mean ignoring profitability. 'The market is divided between individual investors, to whom the moral dimension is usually slightly more important, and institutional investors, to whom the link between SRI and long-term value may usually be more significant. But as a general rule, hardly any investor is ready to relinquish investment profitability.'

Chaos

The final, and arguably the most important, driver of change is a crisis – 'chaos', in Mr Christensen's terminology. Said he, 'You need chaos for there to be development rather than stagnation. You need a shock to the system to galvanise people into changing their behaviour.'

Others agreed that complacency requires a crisis, major or minor, to trigger change. 'If nothing goes wrong, humans feel no need to change,' as Dr Diggelmann put it.

For Mr Biedermann, 'Those huge golden parachutes for CEOs after a takeover are a small example – people can't understand it!' He is hopeful that investors' outrage will lead to a toning down of such packages. On a broader level, however, he added, 'I'm not sure there will be only progress in coming years. There could be some new crisis. Ten years on, I am optimistic, but it won't be a smooth linear path.'

Concluding the discussion on change drivers, Mr Christensen posed a question to the group: 'Do we think in the next ten years there will be another chaos event on the level of 9/11 with its impact on US policies and society?' Most answered yes.

Leaders of change

Who are the players who will lead the change, and what changes in their own roles are likely? In particular, how do the various players help to raise awareness of actual or potential social and environmental problems?

Companies

Businesses themselves will play a role because of reputational risk and the wish to improve their image or brand. But they will also be responding to outside pressures.

'The levers of power are not just big companies whose actions are reported in the newspapers,' said Mr Biedermann. 'There are also many other economic agents, starting with smaller companies (which create 80 per cent of new jobs), NGOs and so forth. Civil society should awake – there is a potential here for change, if people understand that they are in the centre of it all.'

'In ten years,' urged Ms Hodess, 'business has to be more outspoken in terms of societal leadership. Some business leaders will drive change within their company, form alliances with others in the industry, and serve as models that generate peer pressure.'

'Certainly companies are driving awareness,' said Mr Christensen, 'because it's in their interests.'

Of course, Enron and its ilk have raised awareness too, as negative models. Raphael Jaquet of KPMG made this point in his paper for the conference. 'Enron, WorldCom, Parmalat ... to name a few of the most spectacular crises that have affected thousands of employees, customers, suppliers, creditors and investors.

These crises raised questions through the regulators, the business community and the media about the role of the governing bodies of the companies and of the accounting firms.'

Shareholders

Fifty years ago, Mr Biedermann recalled, most shares were held by individuals. Today, more than half are held by institutional investors – pension funds, insurance companies, mutual funds etc. 'This is a big difference, because institutional shareholders are bigger, well organised, know what they are speaking of and represent beneficiaries in whose interest they act. In effect, the general public is intervening in companies through institutional shareholders.'

His foundation, Ethos, is a prime example of this new 'fiduciary capitalism' (and of SRI), managing assets for eighty-five Swiss pension funds according to sustainable development criteria and a systematic exercise of all shareholders' voting and other rights. In his paper for the workshop, he explained that these large investors 'usually invest in a lot of companies, often in a passive (indexed) way. This makes them captive investors, since they can't sell their shares. If they are not satisfied by a company's results, they have no other choice than to become active shareholders.' Moreover, they exercise their voting rights according to the principles of SRI. 'For long-term investors such as pension funds, the financial performance of their investments is important. But in a long-term perspective, a financial performance can't be achieved without simultaneous and great attention to the effects of the companies' activities on their stakeholders: the traditional stakeholders – the employees, clients, suppliers, civil society – and the dummy stakeholders – the natural environment and future generations.'

Mr Biedermann believes that in ten years' time the public will have enough awareness to be putting pressure on fund managers because of mounting interest in how their investment is making for a better society, through better companies. 'Everyone in Switzerland has a pension fund. Now people realise that through their savings they can influence companies. Beneficiaries will become more aware, forcing fund managers to intervene.'

This increased awareness of 'value creation' on behalf of beneficiaries will fuel the trend towards growing shareholder activism as a response to bad management practices. This will shift how managers might believe and behave. As Ms Girard Zappelli said, 'There are already some examples of minority shareholders of large companies who tried to interfere, not always successfully but at least tried. This makes management think, "Oh, maybe there's a problem here, maybe we have to have another way of working," even if it's not a question of ethical values but just the financial performance of the company.'

For Mr Biedermann, the huge golden parachutes for CEOs after a takeover are 'scandalous'. Ms Krasna suggested that such excesses might be tamed 'if people in your position ask for a change in the by-laws, so that board remuneration is voted by the annual shareholders' meeting – and I see signs that this is what is coming. The activists who have enough shares are going to band together to get a motion through the shareholders' meeting. We will see a shift of decision to the individual members. Looking forward, boards are going to lose some of their decision-making power because shareholders are unhappy with how it is being exercised – independent board members not standing up to management. They are going to use pension funds etc. That one can be solved in ten years.'

In ten years, concluded Mr Christensen, shareholders will have more power. 'That's a big change.'

Institutions

If they do their job properly, institutions can help bring about better performance by others. Ms Girard Zappelli said, 'National and international institutions are responsible for raising awareness of problems that need to be addressed.' Thus the United Nations climate change programme, from which the Kyoto Protocol emerged, has increased awareness of that worrisome problem.

Sometimes the problems that need to be addressed are internal. Ms Girard Zappelli's own organisation, the IOC, has done much to clean up its act since 1998, when a scandal broke over bribery charges against the bid committee for the 2002 Olympic Winter Games at Salt Lake City. Among other steps, visits by IOC members to candidate cities have been abolished; greater financial transparency has been ensured through the publication of financial reports on the sources and uses of the Olympic movement's income (the IOC distributes 92 per cent of the revenue generated by TV rights and the marketing of Olympic properties to its national affiliates around the world); and the newly created IOC Ethics Commission, which she represents, has adopted an IOC code of ethics.

Some participants expressed dissatisfaction with the performance of other international institutions – the UN, IMF and World

Bank. 'From the perspective of many NGOs,' said Ms Hodess, 'the international financial institutions haven't made economic globalisation work for the south. The UN system isn't an effective administrator. If we're talking about global adjustments to fix processes that can't be fixed nationally, you need global forces that work better than the ones we have now – without necessarily going to global government.'

Mr Christensen pointed out that UN and other international institutions 'do have a role in providing guidelines and principles, which allows change advocates within an organisation to claim more credibility. So they will have a role, as long as they don't lose their own credibility.' The World Bank, of course, is more directly involved in terms of determining investments.

Media: use and abuse

With the spread of mass communications, the media have enormous power. 'The media create pressure by exposing unethical behaviour and raising awareness and stimulating discussion of global problems that need to be addressed,' said Ms Girard Zappelli.

But she herself, and other participants, raised some criticisms of the media, saying they too often oversimplify issues and miss their long-term significance. Dr Diggelmann spoke of the danger of the media misusing their power. 'The more the power of the media, and the increasing concentration of that power, the greater the danger of misuse. The need for ethical reflection becomes more urgent.' Another danger, said Mr Jaquet, is that the media can sometimes be manipulated.

On balance, concluded Ms Girard Zappelli, 'The media play a crucial role in transmitting information and awakening civil society to its responsibilities. But the media also have to be responsible.'

One change over the next ten years will be a proliferation of new channels. 'The structure of the media is changing,' noted Ms Hodess, referring to 'the importance of the web in terms of dissemination of information, if not always accurate or reliable. This huge new source of information is bound to have an effect.' But she remains optimistic about the future of newspapers. 'Journalism will always attract people who want to poke and ask questions and provoke.'

Governments

Ms Hodess, like other participants, has a jaundiced view of governments in general. 'What I am concerned about in terms of promoting ethical performance,' she said, 'is political life. Who wants to be a politician these days? They are unpopular among the citizenry, subject to opaque party discipline, scrabbling for funds, so what kind of support can we expect from politicians and governments in terms of promoting long-termism? So much dynamism is coming from the private sector, but it's not the private sector's job to care about society.'

The consensus was that governments will have to rebuild trust and credibility, to improve their performance by integrating new values. 'They will have to change because of pressure, even if it is hard,' said Ms Girard Zappelli. 'It may take more than two generations.'

NGOs

NGOs have become important because people have lost trust in government. If our group is correct, in future they will be asked to be not just awareness-raisers but also problem-solvers – but will they be able to retain their NGO status if they are part of the solution?

'NGOs will have to grow up in the coming years,' said Ms Girard Zappelli. 'They have part of the responsibility for improving ethical performance. It is not only companies and institutions that are responsible.'

Ms Hodess expressed the NGOs' viewpoint: 'Transparency International is an awareness-raising NGO,' she said. 'We raise awareness about the dangers of corruption. But is that enough? We need to be part of suggesting solutions. Some NGOs could do that, but not all – they would lose credibility in one of their important functions: finding a cause and promoting that cause.'

Beth Krasna put the question directly: 'If an NGO like TI says, "We track, we show the world," is it also accountable for trying to make them improve? Is transparency enough – are you going to try to take one step more?'

'What we need to do – and it's a huge challenge,' replied Ms Hodess, 'is to show a better way forward, to identify best practice. But my fear is to what extent the public sector will lean on NGOs to perform. Putting too many hopes on civil society is problematic, because NGOs lack the resources of governments; they are not elected and they don't always have the proper accountability. They must be clear about where they get their money, who their sponsors are. So NGOs cannot be problem-solvers or replace governments. We still need a state or a public system – it has resources, budgets, we pay taxes. If we don't rely on the public system to fix itself, to react to the provocations from NGOs or the public, then what is it there for at all?'

Consumers

Consumers will play a role in integrating a new definition of performance. In future they will be more educated and aware.

'In the past,' said Mr Biedermann, 'consumers bought goods on the basis of price and quality. Today we are also looking at where and how they are produced. Nike is a prime example: consumers became aware of children producing Nike shoes because NGOs and the media brought it to public attention. Another example: more than half the bananas sold in Switzerland today are "fair trade" bananas.'

Mr Christensen raised the question of whether such issues will concern just an elite of 'bleeding hearts', or whether this activism will become a mass-market phenomenon. On a ten-year timescale, he concluded, 'It's fair to say this will continue to grow, but we don't know how much.'

Academics

'Academia is also part of raising awareness and suggesting solutions,' Dr Diggelmann reminded us, adding, 'In academia, certain individuals are more important as drivers of change than the institutions that employ them.'

But in future, it was suggested, ethics research will gain a higher profile and will not only be contained within small groups within universities, but institutions might actually start researching this issue. Already, said Ms Krasna, 'Some of the business schools are mainstreaming ethical issues – they are going to devote the first two weeks of the MBA course to ethics and no other subject.'

A concluding comment by Ms Girard Zappelli: 'All these players have to work together, impacting on each other. It is not always easy to decide who will lead the change and how.'

5

Ethics and disobedience

Fiona Fleck

- Disobedience: a moral duty?
  - a form of obedience to a higher moral order
  - a constructive form of protest to bring about social change
- Whistle-blowing: a civic duty?
  - a challenge to group norms
  - rejection, reprisals, punishment or protection
- Nurturing disobedience
  - through dialogue: tolerance in the face of diversity
  - by speaking out: moral courage to blow the whistle
  - by educating the young: how to think and not what to think
  - through communication: information is free

Why disobedience?

The rise of Muslim fundamentalist terror culminating in the 11 September 2001 attacks on the United States and the US-led invasion of Iraq in 2003 have plunged the world into a deep moral crisis and triggered soul-searching to find a new set of shared values that correspond to our fast-changing world.

In that search for commonality, disobedience can play a role as a catalyst for change, but, amid growing chaos, how do we use disobedience to challenge the system and bring about change? How can disobedience help us to find new shared values in our individualised and multicultural society?

Chaos and disorder are within our society. Disobedience, both malign and benign, is part of human nature. Rebellion is in our nature, and unless we control it and submit to order for the common good, chaos will prevail. We may ignore order out of selfishness or greed, as well as tribal or sectarian values, and will be persuaded to submit to order only if we recognise the value of a sound ethical code. From where are the younger generations getting their moral values and what has become of the moral education once provided by religious bodies? It is not always clear what the common values are and whether there are indeed any such values in our society, and that makes peaceful coexistence difficult to achieve.

The main goals and achievements of morality are to prevent conflict and contribute to the settlement of conflict. In a changing, individualised and multicultural society – the 'global village' – where confrontation is on the rise, conflict resolution is of paramount importance.

Conflicts and confrontation result from differences in interests, in religion and in ideologies – sometimes of the most radical kind – between groups or individuals. Traditional values, such as the authority of established religion, that of the Church or the

Mosque, are being undermined. Once beliefs are shared they are codified and enforced by society in laws. Because of changing circumstances, these values cannot be eternal or immutable, but there are constants, such as murder and theft, which are prohibited by every society. However, even these constants are open to interpretation: for example, when killing or theft is sanctioned in a 'just' war.

The role of disobedience in shaping these values is to break the moral code, reset it and re-establish a new code that is relevant to today's society. History shows how societies have always discarded one order in favour of another more relevant one. For example, the Roman Empire became Christian and absorbed paganism. Then, after the Black Death wiped out much of the population in Europe, the new middle class broke away from the rule of the Hapsburgs and the Catholic Church, and that led to the Reformation. In contrast, paganism was stamped out in the Middle East initially leaving a moral and spiritual vacuum. In the eighteenth century the French took religion out of the state to banish the Church as a 'shadow of God on earth' and secularism became the new commonality in that society.

Diverse societies agree that there are constants and that we need these in our moral code, but disagree on the bedrock: the principles that underlie what unites us. To achieve a peaceful coexistence this needs to be established, but how can we achieve this when even the most basic principles can be challenged? The basic principle of ownership for example, challenged by the eighteenth-century German philosopher Ludwig Feuerbach who believed that 'private property' is 'theft'. Similarly, is the economic disparity between the 'haves' and the 'have-nots' God-given or man-made?

Order and chaos
The growing gap between the West and the Muslim world in terms of respect, accepting differences and working together is a challenge to humanity's search for a peaceful, meaningful coexistence. Moreover, insecurity and instability are on the increase across the world.

Since the Second World War, immigration to wealthy industrialised countries has brought together many diverse communities with different values, and this close cohabitation can lead to conflict, underscoring the need for a new set of shared values. Some immigrant populations have remained in ghettos, while others have integrated into society. Some groups have left an indelible mark and are changing the host nation. This clash of cultures raises fundamental questions: what is an acceptable and what an unacceptable minority right, and how should these be defended?

Europe has also faced threats to its stability through terrorism from groups such as Baader-Meinof in Germany and the Red Brigades in Italy, the Irish Republican Army (IRA) in Ireland and ETA, the Basque separatists, in Spain.

The growing phenomenon of 'failed states' in the developing world is another kind of chaos. Several dozen states have collapsed in recent years because of corrupt leaders, war and poverty, as well as foreign support for rebel forces to destabilise that state. The result is a state that can no longer perform its basic functions: the provision of education, security, health care and governance etc. Within this vacuum, people may fall prey to competing factions, crime and corruption, and sometimes the United Nations or neighbouring states have to intervene to try to prevent a humanitarian catastrophe.

To people living in a country like Somalia, Afghanistan or Sierra Leone, where there is virtually no state, it is a daily struggle for survival. Given the hierarchy of survival needs, such as food, shelter, work and health care, ethical concerns may seem like a luxury. Furthermore, Afghanistan and recently Iraq have provided fertile breeding ground for terrorists. There is no reason to think that other collapsed states will not provide new havens in future.

Another form of chaos on the rise is urban lawlessness and violence. A growing number of cities, even in well-functioning states such as Brazil, are giving way to daily insecurity, with increasing numbers of people choosing to live in gated enclaves. In some countries the police lose control of the streets at night; in others people are more afraid of the police than of criminal gangs who keep order. Do governments have the will or the ability to tackle this chaos and reinstate order? Or will the 'Brazilianisation' of cities become the norm?

We don't want to live with conflict, confrontation and instability. There is a pressing need to establish a new order out of this chaos, a new moral order.

The limitations of law
In many societies today, people of different faiths and beliefs live side by side. Those societies in turn reflect what is happening on a global level: the world has become smaller, throwing diverse

religious, ethnic and cultural groups closer together than ever before.

Against this backdrop of clashing systems and conflicting norms, the UN is one of many bodies seeking to develop international standards. The idea is worthy: to get member states to agree on one set of rules. But to achieve consensus is not easy, and even when states do agree on the provisions of international law, some then flout these at will and there is little capacity to police breaches by the lawmakers themselves.

Virtually every nation has signed up to the principles enshrined in the Universal Declaration of Human Rights, and yet there remains much diversity in their interpretation. Furthermore, the principles can be misused. Countries such as China are regularly censured for human rights abuses, but the abuse of detainees in Iraq shows what happens when countries such as the United States and Britain, which view themselves as guardians of human rights, suspend moral judgement.

The Guantanamo detention centre represents a clear suspension of international law and of moral values, yet few Christian and Jewish groups in the United States have taken a principled stand and protested against it. The media there has paid little attention to what protests there are and the general public seem to be unaware or apathetic. In contrast, the legal team at the White House has been up in arms about what it knows is a breach of law.

Educated, legal-minded people are angry about Guantanamo and many aspects of the US-led military campaign in Iraq. Despite much debate, there appears to have been no way to stop the Bush administration from pushing ahead with its radical security policy, particularly after President George W. Bush was re-elected in 2004 by a small majority, 51 per cent of US voters, which in turn raised the question: is the majority always right?

Despite deep concern about the ability of Washington to flout the terms of the Geneva Conventions at the Guantanamo detention centre and in Iraq, few religious and political leaders have taken a moral stand and tried to challenge the government. This underscores a moral dilemma: is it justified to put aside one's morals temporarily when a state is at war and under attack? One answer would be that if it was wrong to do this in two world wars, why should it be right now? This suspension of moral values and violation of international laws has deeply split the global community and made all the more pressing the need for shared values. Amid this chaos, disobedience can act as a catalyst to reinforce values or establish a whole new moral code.

Morals come first and, once there is consensus, they are codified into law, which is in turn enforced. Unlike the legal system, the moral system demands that conscience play a role. This means that you can be legally wrong but morally right. By disobeying the law, you obey something else: a higher ethical order. Disobedience is a form of obedience; in disobeying one thing you obey another. The eighteenth-century Irish political philosopher Edmund Burke famously summed up this moral imperative: 'All it takes for evil men to succeed is for good men to do nothing.'

But how do we know when and what action to take to stop 'evil men' from succeeding? When is it right to disobey the law, our parents, our boss or any other authority for sound ethical reasons and how can this help us to challenge and change the system?

Disobedience: a form of moral courage

Crime or law-breaking is a refusal of order, while benign disobedience is morally motivated. A criminal rejects order, while a disobedient person might break the law on one point in order to obey his or her conscience. That person's conscience obeys a moral code which is formed by individual, societal, religious, political and other factors. How we are commanded to act is made up of a complex of historical and other factors which shape our sense of place in society. As members of a family, community, nation and global human family, our behaviour is guided by this code and sanctions for disobedience – failure to follow the code – are part of this code.

Unfortunately, commandments to obey do not always align with each other. We may be called upon by one authority to obey against the dictates of our conscience. That authority almost always comes with a wrapping of justification in moral or other terms which can put us in direct conflict with the demands of another authority. Hence our own personal belief system, whether this is formed individually or something we have bought into institutionally, may cause us to obey one authority and not another, each with claims on us as human beings, believers or citizens.

For instance, a religious belief in the sanctity of life and the admonition against taking life may require a Quaker to refuse a command to take up arms or pay taxes to buy arms or fight a war. In some countries, conscientious objection to military service or the right to refuse to take up arms is codified in the law itself. In other countries, it is a criminal offence.

Under international law, we are required by an agreed and codified global ethic to obey certain principles. And we can – especially since the International Criminal Court started its work in 2003 – be held accountable if we breach this law.

It is difficult to say whether a planetary ethic, one that takes account of the rights and well-being of humans and other life forms, is emerging. Some would argue that the failure to obey such an ethic by correcting trends such as global warming puts not only ourselves but future generations in jeopardy, which is something we do not have a right to do. In some cases, people are so committed to these larger imperatives – beyond individual and national interests – that they feel compelled to break the existing civil law: for example, to join global trade demonstrations or damage military property.

This decision to disobey one authority in favour of a greater cause – a superior ethic or moral imperative – is the decisive factor in ethical disobedience.

Do the ends justify the means?

There is a large grey area defining what disobedience may or may not be, encompassing terrorism, the use of force and violent protest. An individual in this situation believes that there is no choice but to reinstate moral values through force. This raises the question of whether the ends justify the means and underscores a more fundamental problem with ethics and disobedience: that when a new ethic takes hold by means of a disobedient action or gesture, it often carries within it the seeds of a new oppressive system.

Within a few years of standing up to the Pope and bringing about the Reformation, Europe's great religious revolution, Luther became a champion of the aristocracy and corrupted himself. The Islamic Revolution in Iran overthrew the Shah of Iran and promised more social equity but heralded a new form of tyranny.

Recognising this is not new. When Maximilien Robespierre and other French revolutionaries fell victim to the new regime they had fought to install, the eighteenth-century writer Pierre Vergniaud famously commented, 'Revolution is like Saturn, it eats its own children.' Must chaos come first before order is established? Does change – albeit necessary change – have to be so painful? What steps can be taken to make necessary change more evolutionary?

Enormous social changes have been brought about without violence. For example, the primary education system in the United Kingdom since the Second World War, the American civil rights movement and women's fight for the vote.

What ways are there of dealing with conflict without resorting to violence? Many groups are involved in reducing the widespread availability of small arms and light weapons to prevent violence, loss of life and the impact they have on communities. One solution is to restrict the sale of small arms, but this is not so simple in places such as the Balkans, where weapons are part of the culture, and where people keep them for self-defence.

Some groups resort to violence to voice their concerns and protest about unfairness: for example, some Asian youths who rioted in northern English cities at the recent election of an overtly racist British National Party candidate were well-educated graduates who said they could only get jobs in restaurants or as taxi drivers. Young people are being alienated, with explosive results, in Western societies and unless they can be given a platform to air their grievances, there may be more street violence.

Children today are influenced by movies and video games in which violence is a banal, daily occurrence and force is a common solution to conflict. In extreme cases, children have been involved in shoot-outs at their own schools. Adolescents are growing up in an environment where violence appears to be socially acceptable. It is as if violence has become orthodox and non-violence – or the rejection of force – unorthodox. In such a world, Quaker non-violent video games – if they existed – would be a form of benign disobedience.

The world wants to move towards universal ethics, a shared moral code, and yet since the 11 September 2001 attacks on the United States it has been veering towards even more terror, violence and hatred. Terrorism in the form of suicide attacks is a particular challenge because people who are not afraid to die cannot be threatened; they must be won over. Violence does not have the power to change hate and prejudice, anger and arrogance, hopelessness, frustration and fear, or to bring justice, freedom and peace. In short, you have to convince people who resort to violence that dialogue is by far preferable and that force is not the answer to any issue.

Are suicide bombers obeying their conscience or have they been manipulated by others who are not prepared to give their lives for a cause? One person's freedom fighter is another person's terrorist. Postmodern theologians are disturbed by the fact that they are quickly surrounded by people who, in religious terms, know everything. Truth can easily be used by charlatans as a smoke screen. In religion, the fanatics are those who say, 'I am so good, I am obeying all the rules, I am better than you,' and use their presumed moral rectitude to manipulate others.

Fanatics can also be people running governments who take a radical view of justice and punish disobedience as a crime. They say, 'Justice is so important and must prevail, so we have to kill people for this.' But the ends do not justify the means. Fanaticism is infantile. The contrast is a society that is mature enough to accommodate disobedience and authorities that are mature enough to provide education and engage in dialogue.

Disobedience as non-violent resistance

Disobedience means taking a principled stand as a conscientious objector or a whistle-blower and can mean engaging in diverse forms of civil disobedience, such as peaceful street protests or cyber-activism. Many people are afraid of conflict and prefer to avoid confrontation. The idea of conflict often meets with wholesale rejection by peace campaigners and religious groups, and leads to a discussion of whether conflict can provide the means to a good end. There is no doubt that some rules and laws become outdated and may need revision. Conflict, if used constructively, can help to challenge the status quo. In some situations there is little alternative to conflict because people and societies often change only under pressure.

Certain acts of civil disobedience stand out as iconic, particularly those of a non-violent nature: think, for example, of Mahatma Gandhi's campaigns against the British Empire that contributed towards Indian independence in 1947; the peaceful protests by Burmese opposition leader Au Sang Suu Kyi; the Chinese student standing defiant in front of a tank on Tiananmen Square in 1989. In all of these, non-violence is one of the fundamental principles guiding civil disobedience and something that some groups, notably the Quakers, have codified in their faith.

Is it acceptable to go outside the limits and resort to violence when democracy fails? There is a trend towards more violence when this seems the only way to capture media attention as a means to achieving a just end. Restriction – voluntary or coerced – of media coverage is not the answer, because this may also restrict a just cause. Moreover, with the advent of the Internet this is no longer realistic. Anyone can use web technology to air just about any view. This raises further issues, such as the difficulty the public faces in evaluating levels of objectivity, accuracy and quality of information in the digital sphere when there are no editorial parameters or controls. Faced with such a massive, disordered flow of information, how can the public decide whether their ethical choices are free or being manipulated by others?

Disobedience means standing up to an authority that bases its power on principles perceived to be no longer valid by an intelligent community. That is what Luther did in bringing about the Reformation. But how do you stop constructive disobedience from being corrupted once it achieves power? How do you wean people from power and authority and make power so diffuse that it can not be abused?

The Orange Revolution in the Ukraine in 2004 is one of the most important social changes in recent history because it was non-violent. Where did the people learn non-violence? The Orange Revolution is a sign that something has taken hold: openness, accessibility and a natural connectedness with the rest of the world. The key to this change was communication. People were brought closer together in their campaign for a free and fair democratic election through technology: mobile phones and cyber-activism. Such use of technology allows people to communicate, connect and organise in real time and at low cost, thus increasing the effectiveness of disobedience activities. Such technologies are likely to be used increasingly in future to enable benign disobedience because they are cost-effective and highly efficient.

Whistle-blowers face moral dilemma

The individual who is disobedient and blows the whistle on an Enron, where a senior accountant alerted the chief executive to an accounting fraud, or an Arthur Andersen, where employees set up a whistle-blowing hotline, may be ethically correct but possibly in breach of the workplace code. Such an individual faces a dilemma between identifying with and belonging to a group with cohesive rules and speaking out from his or her conscience.

Fear of rejection or reprisals and for a person's professional future is a powerful reason for not stepping out of line to take a moral stand. Failure to do so, however, could have even worse implications, not just for the individual but for the organisation and even society as a whole.

The whistle-blower starts off as part of a social group with rules and norms without which the group would not exist and by which the group is guided.

But if that person finds the group's norms inadequate, how does he or she influence the group to scale up the minority view to that of the majority? Does that person remain in the group and try to change the norms, or does he or she leave to establish another group with a better set of norms?

We are already seeing that the fragmentation of clashing groups, interests and ethical codes is increasing. This is also due to a growing failure to recognise authority and the multiplicity of ethical codes. In this situation, power is no longer the preserve of a single authority but takes the form of peer pressure to conform to the group ethic. Another kind of fragmentation is the self-service approach to a group moral code where, for example, a Catholic may select aspects of the Church that suit him or her, while rejecting its stand on, say, abortion and use of condoms to fight HIV/AIDS.

The dilemma for the whistle-blower is where to go to air his or her concerns? In stepping out of line, individuals risk running into the arms of the wrong people, such as those who claim a monopoly on the truth. These may be fundamentalists, suicide sects and groups such as the Scientologists. Terrorist groups may share the whistle-blower's ideals too, but there may be a compromise involved when, for example, they run prostitution, gun and drug rackets to finance their activities.

Whether a whistle-blower is punished or protected will have much to do with group culture, which also determines whether to engage in dialogue with the person. In order to do this, the group needs to accept the challenge and be prepared to change the rules. A group needs to see the benefit of whistle-blowers, understanding that such people should not be treated as martyrs or traitors and ostracised by the group; rather, their contribution to the group should be seen as constructive, and as a civic duty. Groups need to nurture this form of benign disobedience for their own good.

How to nurture benign disobedience

How do you nurture constructive disobedience capable of bringing about the right kind of change and what is the price? How do you challenge the death penalty or arms sales by disobedience in a society that otherwise agrees it is wrong to kill? How do you ensure that you have institutions that are robust enough to accommodate the whole spectrum from prohibition to permissiveness, in countries ranging from Saudi Arabia to Sweden. How does society accommodate and nurture disobedience?

One of the challenges is to prepare people for disobedience. Building moral courage requires skills and people need to be prepared to face being ostracised initially and, in extreme cases, persecuted by society.

Four avenues for nurturing disobedience were identified.

1. Through dialogue

Society needs to keep the communications lines open to those who step out of line, from the whistle-blowers and the political dissidents to the terrorists. This requires maturity and involves a tolerance or acceptance of diversity.

Efforts to resolve the conflict in Northern Ireland took a huge leap forward when the then British prime minister, John Major, was able to talk to the terrorists, displaying a maturity not shown by the hardliners. It is this kind of approach that is also needed for dealing with disobedience. A lesser-known example is that of Judge Hamoud al-Hitar of Yemen and four other Islamic scholars who recently convinced al-Qaeda prisoners that their violent terror campaign was wrong through weeks of theological debate.

Education, especially a philosophical education, can contribute to using reason instead of resorting to violence to solve conflicts. The main obstacle to using reason is bad philosophy, which can limit our capacity to communicate by obscuring language and preaching relativism, racism, nationalism, tribalism or any other kind of particularism.

The main task of good philosophy is to facilitate communication and, in particular, the discussion of important problems, particularly moral problems generated by conflicting interests, using rational arguments.

A precondition of such dialogue is that we speak the same language, but first of all we must understand the questions we are trying to answer. Only then can we reason with one another, producing arguments that both parties can understand, and together scrutinise those arguments to see which are good and which are bad. This was what Socrates was doing when he started the business of philosophy.

2. By speaking out

The key function of disobedience is to speak out against wrong or evil, to name and shame, to take a principled stand and to show moral courage. This inevitably sets the individual on a collision course with the prevailing authority. How does an individual decide whether moral courage is required, and when to step out of line and speak out?

For example, is it morally right to obey or disobey orders in the military?

The defence 'I was just following orders' used in the Nuremberg trials after the Second World War and recently in the investigation into events at Abu Ghraib prison in Baghdad, where US soldiers abused detainees, was clearly unacceptable. You have to obey lawful orders, but how do you know as an ordinary soldier whether an order is lawful or not? It's hard to believe that individual soldiers did not know that the humiliation and abuse of prisoners at Abu Ghraib was wrong. In the end, someone summoned up the moral courage to speak out and report the abuse. In future, the integrity of each soldier will become increasingly important, with more onus on the individual to be clear about what is lawful or not, what is right or wrong in the military. The means to speak out with all the technology available may be much easier than it has been in the past, but whether such people step forward depends a great deal on how whistle-blowers are treated.

Conscientious objection is another example of disobedience in the military. By refusing to take up arms and do military service a person is obeying his or her conscience. But if the society to which that individual belongs faces an enemy that wants to destroy it, mass refusal to go to war could be suicidal. What would have happened if the Second World War allies had not taken up arms against Nazi Germany and other Axis countries?

The international community has the means to decide whether a war is just through the UN. But not all member states are prepared to recognise the UN, with all its diverse interest groups, as the moral authority capable of deciding this. Moreover, sometimes member states take a selective approach: for example, the US with its campaign in Iraq, which started in March 2003 without UN backing.

Terrorism is a major challenge to our collective well-being and needs to be fought with the same means it uses to convince and recruit young men and women. A war or conflict fought in the name of religion needs to be condemned by religious leaders. Al-Qaeda insists it is fighting to reinstate a purer form of Islam, and for that reason it is the duty of Muslims to speak out against the group's violent attacks. If Islamic leaders were more forthright in their condemnation of al-Qaeda, fewer frustrated young Muslim idealists would be drawn to the movement.

During the conflict in Northern Ireland, few religious and political groups in the United States condemned the killing and terrorist attacks, although these leaders may have carried considerable moral authority. Some Church leaders in the United Kingdom also lacked the moral courage to condemn the killings for fear of losing support and alienating their own communities.

In some ways, terrorism can be seen as the war of the poor. Poor people today have enough information to know they are poor. The growing disparity between rich and poor is an explosive situation that can only become worse in the next ten years. Under certain circumstances, when people are denied a share of resources and lack all forms of power, including access to the media, they naturally resort to protest. Protest, of which terrorism is a form, can be justified, but there is a giant fissure down the middle of terrorism. On one side there is the African National Congress (ANC), which fought with both peaceful and violent means to end apartheid in South Africa, and on the other side the extreme terrorists, like al-Qaeda.

A suicide bomber is in a different category from the whistle-blower. The whistle-blower in a big company risks being punished by the bosses and ostracised by colleagues, while a suicide bomber is considered a hero and that person's family is financially rewarded by the society in which he or she lived. Psychologically, it may be much more difficult to be a whistle-blower than a suicide bomber. It is easier to participate in moral courage as part of a group than as an individual.

In other contexts, such as the business world, there is also a need for taking a moral stand. In retrospect, everyone agrees it was right to blow the whistle on accounting fraud at Enron and Arthur Andersen. But how can you nurture the moral courage or disobedience needed for employees to blow the whistle on less clearly defined workplace ills, such as harassment and bullying?

Some companies are already tackling this challenge. For example, Citigroup has elected to provide mandatory training in ethics for all employees. The trend is towards organisations and corporations stepping in to provide the ethical training and moral guidance once provided by the Church, families and communities.

3. By educating the young

From where are younger generations getting their moral values and what has become of the moral education once provided by religious bodies? Stable societies provide a moral education with the values of the group transferred to children, but problems arise when these values are contradictory, or when some members of the group uphold them while others do not.

Is a stable society the precondition for a moral education, or is a moral education first needed for a stable society? With increased immigration and mobility that bring together groups with diverse and often conflicting values, there is no longer one moral education but many kinds. In Western democracies there is a libertarian view that resists the idea of imposing a moral education. The result is that many children no longer receive any and are looking elsewhere for their values.

In the absence of an alternative, young people may get their values from popular culture, movies, video games and television, where many of the role models are not good: for example, Michael Jackson, who has been on trial for child sex offences. Furthermore, public trust in authority, such as governments, is diminished when people see how President Bush and Tony Blair lied to their citizens over Iraq's weapons of mass destruction (WMD) capability and used this as a pretext to go to war.

One place young people are and will increasingly be getting their values from is peer groups, which are replacing figures of authority. The question is: how does an intelligent community influence peer-group norms? In future it is likely that social movements, peace organisations and human rights groups are going to have a greater influence on society and on reinforcing moral values. They are going to step in where politicians have lost public trust and confidence, and failed in this task. They have increasing influence and, through technology, the means to propagate this. But it is uncertain whether peer groups can provide a moral education. A moral education should undoubtedly evolve towards not just telling the young what is right and wrong, but teaching them how to make such decisions for themselves.

In future, education is likely to be carried out more and more by professional bodies, such as corporations and large organisations, which, in order to maintain their reputations, will need to ensure that each individual adheres to the ethical policy of the body in question. To do that, they will increasingly need to provide training and education.

Schools too would benefit from offering a moral education, not perhaps necessarily in the traditional form of religious studies, given today's multiplicity of beliefs and faiths, but rather by teaching the young how to think and not necessarily what to think. One solution would be to include philosophy and debate in the school curriculum. This would give children the means to solve moral questions by themselves later in life.

4. Through communication
The Internet is a great social experiment with a rationalist core

needed to make it function. Early theorists said it was essentially antithetical to censorship. They argued that the Internet interpreted censorship as damage and routed around it, but this has a downside. The impact of giving a free platform to criminal and neo-Nazi groups who are not attacking the functions of the Internet but rather using these to attack social consensus can have a destabilising effect on society. There is no choice but to take action against incitement to racial and other kinds of hatred.

Some governments have found ways to control Internet content. China, for example, maintains a firewall around the nation to rein in non-orthodoxy, but these attempts are always provisional, as is often the case with the web. The Internet has broken chains in societies where official censors routinely vetted personal letters, such as in Egypt and Pakistan. The Internet is a vital tool to support civil disobedience. It has already helped peaceful transition to democracy in the Ukraine. Many countries have recognised that this newly found digital freedom means that children are more easily exposed to pornography and have taken steps to protect them.

Stewart Brand, a libertarian theorist and the co-founder of Global Business Network, said, 'Information wants to be free.' It is difficult, if not impossible, to reverse the freedom of information the Internet has brought society. In terms of information, the cat has truly been let out of the bag.

Standing up to organised political authority is something that can only advance society. But there is no guarantee that, in the age of the mass media, your message – however valid – will be heard. Despite the subversive effect of the Internet, public opinion is still easy to manipulate. Political authorities will always find new ways of manipulating public opinion. For disobedience to succeed, it needs to be sophisticated, and dissenters need to blow their whistles as loud as possible to get the attention they deserve.

Cyber-activism is civil disobedience conducted in the web-sphere, the digital world. The people who engage in it are sometimes the same people who do it in the real world. For them, the Internet is just another forum. There are also cyber-activists who confine their disobedience to the web. In the digital world, there are activists who block websites anonymously too, creating damage to the Internet gratuitously. They represent malign disobedience in the digital sphere. These people reject order, break laws and are destructive, and it is virtually impossible to engage them in constructive dialogue because they cannot be traced.

In contrast, there are also examples of constructive disobedience on the Internet: for example, a UK group that created a website called mysociety.org, which distributes funding to people with disobedient ideas for the Internet. One of these was a website called Fax Your MP, which presents a constructive challenge to authority by allowing people to fax letters of complaint to their Member of Parliament and providing a simple mechanism by which to follow up their complaint. The idea of easy access to the MP and a user-friendly mechanism to contact them can be rolled out for other purposes. This is an effective tool of disobedience because it is constructive and non-violent.

The Internet: a parallel world

Over a billion people or one-sixth of the world's population have access to the Internet. In the digital world everything is in play, new norms are being tried out and it's all about which group and which philosophy will win. There is a technical order in the digital world without which it would not function and that order is jealously guarded by the technicians and geeks. It is what defines the Internet's standards.

The Internet represents a clash of cultures: for example, business vs. anarchy, the owners of intellectual property (IP) vs. the users of IP. Here too there is a struggle to find equilibrium within diversity. Much of the Internet community talks about standards and fiercely defends them against outside forces, usually perceived as big business: for example, Microsoft, which is trying to impose its own standard on the Internet.

Microsoft, like most businesses, makes money by investing in ideas and then jealously protecting them while exploiting them for profit. That is normal in the real world, but in cyberspace it clashes with the pervasive geek orthodoxy that ideas should be distributed for nothing, that open source and free software, for instance, is morally, technically and ecologically better than closed or proprietary software like that developed by Microsoft.

In some ways the defenders of standardisation are right. Standards seem an obvious solution for creating commonality, providing a common language through which diverse people and groups can communicate. However, compliance and standards in the digital world enable communication but tend to iron out diversity. The more we comply with the standards, the more effectively we communicate in the digital sphere. Some people argue that we should invest less in standards and more in translation, so that we can allow a higher degree of diversity on the Internet, or a digital form of peaceful coexistence. This means that a multitude of standards may in future happily coexist thanks to the technology of translation.

Just as in the real world, there are crime and extreme cases of disobedience on the net: for example, hackivism, aberrant behaviour, releasing viruses and bombarding websites with messages. Moreover, the Internet represents many interlocking orthodoxies, some providing help to the authorities or to the underclass, to the obedient or to the disobedient, and even to the anarchists and wreckers. The language of the digital world is redolent of the clash between order and chaos, with key terms such as compliance and standards. The digital world is divided into pro- and anti-standards camps. The Internet is a complex ecology and both models are certain to coexist indefinitely.

The future: using disobedience for ethical purposes

Our globalised and interdependent world is pointing us in different directions. We will have incomplete and often conflicting principles to guide us in the future, as our planet becomes more populated, our environment more polluted and our weapons more deadly, as the world becomes more dangerous and more self-destructive. What are the higher principles which must guide us as a human community, with all our diversities, and where does disobedience come in?

Disobedience can be a constructive form of protest that is vital for bringing change and it will continue as long as people are dissatisfied with the status quo, as long as they feel excluded, powerless and alienated from society.

While young people – for example, young immigrants in Europe – are not included in the sharing of power and resources and do not have a voice, they are more likely to turn to violence and fundamentalist ideology. These people must be encouraged and given the means to put their energies into something positive. As we recognise the diversity of God's creation, we realise that minorities have to have a space, and one that is not imposed by a majority. We need a society based on respect for diversity and one which must find other forms of coexistence, rather than a majority–minority view.

Democratic forms can also nurture constructive disobedience. For example, Lawrence Kohlberg, a psychologist and educator, developed what he called 'moral education through democratic schooling' based on a system of participatory democracy and one person one vote. When introduced in prisons and schools, he found that this approach encouraged individuals to take more responsible for the community as a whole.

Patience is required for disobedience, because change can be slow. The United States saw its biggest peace demonstration in history on 15 February 2003 in New York City, and yet President Bush was still elected by a slim majority for a second term. The protest may not have had an immediate effect but the voters, the opposition and public opinion may slowing be changing.

There are situations where there is going to be a stalemate, where there are conflicting claims. For example, when two groups claim the same piece of land, such as the Palestinians and Israelis. Another stalemate situation is the clash in France between the state that insists on a secular school system and Muslim pupils who wear headscarves as an expression of their religious and cultural identity. Again, there may be no solution.

Such conflicts will lead to a fragmentation where there is a limit to dialogue and commonality, but where the majority view is not going to decide. As people identify with smaller groups, they are going to adhere to the codes of those groups and may not find communality, other than in broad forms such as a ban on murder and theft. In this case, it is not possible to achieve a higher moral order which everyone can share, but perhaps it is possible to find peaceful coexistence with tolerance and acceptance of diversity. Before we find that equilibrium and in this stalemate situation, however, protest forms are likely to remain violent.

Obedience will continue to be a virtue in just institutions and with regard to lawful orders or laws laid down by legitimate authorities. Disobedience is not justified when motivated by sectarian or selfish interests. It is, however, justified and may even be a moral imperative whenever the conditions of justice, legitimacy and lawfulness are not fulfilled.

A disobedient person or a whistle-blower appeals to a higher moral order beyond that person's group or institution. The higher moral order represents norms which every member of a society of equals in a state of equality should obey. Sometimes these norms are already accepted but not adhered to. Sometimes that person discovers and anticipates entirely new norms and brings them into existence by an act of disobedience.

Sometimes disobedience can serve to reinforce the moral order, such as civil disobedience. Where civil disobedience is violent, this can be justified when there is no other alternative and when there is a clear moral principle at stake.

To nurture the kind of disobedience that can reinforce or renew moral norms, people need to develop skills to enable them to analyse a situation in terms of a moral framework.

Moral education aimed at improving moral reasoning and debate will become even more important in the future. But perhaps the most important requirement is to summon up the moral courage to take a principled stand regardless of group pressure or punishment.

6

Ethics in real time

Richard Brass

- New ethical challenges are being faced in particular sectors, such as the media and the military
- Real-time technologies are
  - impacting on decision-making and judging what constitutes reality
  - damaging relationships between organisations and individuals
- Real-time information is
  - destroying trust in organisations and threatening their survival
  - creating confusion and a thirst for new sources of ethical standards

Developments in information and communications technology in recent years have transformed the world. The astonishing advance, both technological and geographical, of the Internet, mobile telephony, wireless communication and digital information systems has made many areas of activity almost unrecognisable to people working in those same fields even as recently as ten years ago.

In the media, the military, medicine, the financial markets and humanitarian organisations the impact of these changes has been profound and challenging. While many of the consequences of the sudden creation of a world in which everything happens in real time, everywhere and at once, are undoubtedly positive, the arrival of this world has brought with it immense pressures on the way organisations and individuals work and respond to each other.

Whether it's the medical devices that influence doctors' life-and-death decisions, the weaponry that requires an immediate and instinctive military response, the live reporting pressures that fixate journalists or the presence in a region in need of humanitarian assistance of a population armed with mobile phones and Internet access, the pressures of the real-time world have not only changed the way this work is done but also challenged the ethical frameworks that have traditionally underpinned this activity. The nature of that challenge is only now becoming apparent, but as the pace of technological change makes real time ever more important, the pressure on ethics is growing ever stronger.

Here, now and everywhere: ethical challenges of real time today

The significance of the ethical challenge posed by real time can be judged from the fact that it is already changing one of the central processes of all human activity. Across all sectors, industries and activities, real-time technology is introducing a fundamental change to the way in which decisions are made.

Traditionally, decision-making has been a process involving analysis and reflection, followed by the crucial moment when the deepest concerns, motivations, convictions, inclinations and habits of the decision-maker are brought to bear and the decision is made. In a world characterised by real-time interactions, this process is changed fundamentally. The discipline imposed by real time means decisions are taken increasingly quickly, severely limiting the amount of analysis and reflection that can be undertaken and which formed the first stage of traditional decision-making. In these changed circumstances, the final decisive moment, informed by instincts, habits and emotions, becomes far more important than it ever was.

Thus, paradoxically, the progress of technology ostensibly bent towards rational ends in fact brings to the fore the importance of instincts, emotions and snap decisions based on essentially non-rational foundations. Where convictions and inclinations are dominant rather than rationality, the ethical base of the decision-maker becomes more important than ever in informing the decision that will finally be made.

The second central change caused by real-time pressures is the trend towards disintermediation. In the past, audiences – not simply media audiences but also the audiences observing or concerned with the activities of all kinds of organisations and individuals – were content to have the information they received passed to them through a process of intermediation, involving some form of selection and combination that can broadly be termed as editing. Whether that came in a news report or in a report from a financial, humanitarian or military organisation, the information was edited and presented by someone else. The ethics of the editor determined which information was transmitted, in what form and what combination, and how it was presented. The ethics of the audience were primarily involved only in the decision about which of relatively few editors to choose as a trustworthy source, and once that decision was made the ethical concerns lay largely with someone else.

In the real-time world people are far less prepared to receive their information in the same way. The exponential growth in the number of sources and in the ways of receiving information in real time has in many people's view made the editing role redundant. Often this is due to a growing expectation of instant gratification and often because the lack of an editor seems to imply purer, more real information. In this disintermediated world, the ethical decisions formerly taken by editors now lie with the audiences themselves. With a plethora of sources of information and forms of communication, audiences must somehow come up with their own ethical basis upon which to make fundamental decisions about what to accept as real and what to reject.

Technology vs. ethics in the news business

The issue of disintermediation is just one of many changes presented by the real-time world to media organisations. These bodies, many of which formerly held an elevated ethical position in the eyes of vast audiences due to their role not only as editors but as editors regarded as ethically robust, are facing a multiplying array of challenges from real time, many of which go to their ethical heart. In order to survive financially and to continue to receive the trust of their audiences, forward-looking media organisations are reassessing their internal and external processes to meet these real-time challenges and adjust to the ethical problems they pose.

Several of the ethical problems caused by real-time developments were highlighted for media organisations during the invasion of Iraq in 2003 and the ensuing occupation. For the first time, television and Internet audiences could literally have a front-row seat at the theatre of war in real time. Although this was broadly understood in theoretical terms, the reality of it came as a severe shock to media organisations in terms of the dilemmas it posed.

In the broadest sense real-time technology caused reputable organisations such as the BBC a problem in terms of trying to present the picture of the war as a whole, against the temptation to show the most dramatic footage as quickly as possible, which can easily give an impression which is at odds with the truth of the larger reality. Before the arrival of the real-time world, the bigger picture would be built from the smaller pieces and then presented, rather than the pieces being presented as they emerged.

The BBC has clear guidelines about how to report an event such as the war in Iraq, but the speed of real-time technology and the fact that BBC content can now instantly be seen anywhere in the world pushed those guidelines to the limit. The organisation then faced a dilemma over questions such as whether to show real-time footage of crowds in Baghdad searching for US pilots who might have been shot down or whether to broadcast footage of kidnappers parading their hostages, balancing freedom of information with the risk of providing the oxygen of publicity to the kidnappers. The BBC finally dealt with these issues by resolving to introduce an element of delay between receiving real-time footage and broadcasting it, during which time considered decisions could be made about the merits of the footage, and by deciding not to broadcast any more scenes of kidnappers with their hostages, a position that was then taken up first by other Western media organisation and later by Arab television channels as well.

These responses were examples of how, in the case of broadcast delays, the ethical problem posed by the arrival of real-time technological possibilities was dealt with by taking a step away from real time, and in the case of the hostages, how an ethical stand by one organisation in opposition to real-time competitive pressures resulted in that ethical position being taken up more widely.

One real-time-related effect of these choices, however, was that in Arab countries, where the BBC's coverage can now be seen just as quickly as in London, the corporation's innate tendency not to show the most grotesque results of war, a long-term ethical practice with a cultural basis, was widely regarded as a sign of pro-coalition bias, particularly when compared with the readiness of other organisations to transmit real-time footage of all kinds. The corporation has had to reflect on its standards to decide whether it may need to show more in future in order to refute this charge, a clear example of an ethical dilemma which, were the BBC's audience not expanded by real-time technology and had the competitive pressures generated by real time not existed, would never have arisen.

Examples of ethical standards changing in the news media under the impact of competitive real-time pressures can be found all over the world, although more often the technology is allowed to drive the ethics, rather than ethics being used to control the technology as in the BBC's case. Broadcasters in Los Angeles recently showed real-time feeds of a man on a freeway shooting at cars and finally killing himself, arguing afterwards that to use a delay to edit out the more troubling scenes would have lost them viewers to their competitors. Even as sober a publication as the *New York Times* is today prepared to show far more graphic images than ten years ago in order to remain competitive in the real-time world. Both cases go to the heart of the ethical impact of real time, and both serve as reminders that the technological capability to do everything live, in real-time, doesn't mean it's the right thing to do.

The collapse of trust

Media organisations are not the only ones whose ethical base is affected by the emergence of an expanded and immediate audience due to the development of real-time technology. In the military world, the identity of the people each soldier has been seeking to influence has traditionally been straightforward: those at the other end of the soldier's gun sights and those nearby. For the individual soldier in an operational situation, there was no need to think about an audience beyond those limits. In the real-time world, however, the activities of soldiers and other military professionals are just as liable to immediate transmission all over the world as any other, being seen by local civilians, citizens of the soldiers' home countries, political controllers, human rights organisations, war crimes prosecutors, the military of other countries and any other interested parties. Even if there's no television crew for miles, there will at least be mobile phones with video capability in the soldiers' own camp, so their activities are now easily open to monitoring and evaluation by people of whom the individual soldier may be completely unaware.

To deal with this development, military organisations and individual soldiers are having to rapidly reprioritise everything they do on the basis of the impact it will have, rather than basing their priorities exclusively on the impact on the traditional audience at the other end of the gun, a considerable ethical shift for both the military organisation as a whole and the individual soldier.

For humanitarian organisations, the arrival of the real-time world is creating a genuine crisis of confidence. This is rooted in the impact real-time technology is having upon people's attitudes towards organisations generally. Where once relations between humanitarian organisations – and others – and the public were characterised by the phrase 'trust me', the availability of immediate and copious information about the activities of organisations all over the world is replacing that with relations characterised by the phrase 'prove it'.

The mission and mandate of organisations such as the International Committee of the Red Cross (ICRC) are rooted entirely in ethics, and their reputation as ethical organisations allows them to carry out work in some of the most dangerous and turbulent parts of the world where it would be impossible if perceptions of the organisation were more negative. The availability of real-time information, however, is changing that situation quickly. News of a failure, scandal or poor result involving one humanitarian organisation in one corner of the world can be all over the world in seconds and have a devastating impact on the perception of that entire organisation in the eyes of its audience of aid recipients, donors, governments and local political elites. Trust in such bodies is therefore evaporating quickly, and the parts of the audience that they need to appeal to in order to do their work are now saying 'prove it' as a prerequisite for providing money or allowing access to areas in need of aid.

This trend, which is causing a reassessment of the ethical basis of such organisations, has been highlighted by recent cases, again connected with Iraq and the Middle East. When the serious abuse of prisoners at the US detention camp at Abu Ghraib came to light, the immediacy of the images and the speed with which they were transmitted and commented upon left organisations such as the ICRC prey to heavy criticism. The ICRC had been working within Abu Ghraib at the time, and in a pre-real-time world the totality of the picture of its work there would have limited such criticism, but the immediate combination of pictures and emotion created a response whose fundamental message was that the ICRC wasn't doing its job.

The global nature of real-time technology is also having a

detrimental effect, forcing humanitarian organisations to make changes that affect their ethical base. The ICRC, for example, would traditionally take responsibility for its people in local areas. If there was a perceived security threat, the organisation would be able to check if the threat was directed against them, check where it was coming from and check if they could continue their work. It could take months, but the work could usually carry on during that time. But when Mullah Omar was quoted on Associated Press as saying that all humanitarian organisations were enemies of Islam, and that statement went all over the world immediately and appeared on the streets of Pakistan, where the ICRC was working, it was much more difficult to manage. The threat was global, very quick, very indirect and impossible to check. Real time breaks the global/local balance.

Reputation, the organisation and the individual

The problems faced by humanitarian organisations highlight the dramatic effect real-time information can have on any organisation's reputation, changing the way the ethics of the organisation relate to the ethics of each individual within it. Information about the actions of one person can be transmitted and disseminated all over the world immediately, with the result that one representative's actions can have a much faster and bigger impact on the entire organisation than ever before. This situation creates a new problem for organisations whose effectiveness and reason for being is based on their ethical reputation. Those organisations become much more inward-looking, shifting the focus away from their relationship with their audience. They are now focusing on the link between the ethics of the organisation and the ethics of the individual representing the organisation. That creates problems for individual autonomy and initiative, which can be crucial to the work of such bodies. Due to real-time pressures, it's no longer enough for humanitarian or other organisations to tell their people to be neutral. Instead these organisations need to be much more concrete, clearer, and much more focussed on best practice. The organisation's priority becomes making sure that its ethics are not only understood by its people but actively put into practice.

This principle can be extended. Organisational culture and the ethics underlying it, which have traditionally been regarded as a problem for management, must become a shared problem. With real-time technology providing the means by which the activities of one person can put the entire organisation at risk, it becomes more important than ever for every member of the organisation to share its ethics and adopt them actively. This poses a significant cultural challenge in organisations in which responsibility for ethics and standards of conduct has traditionally been regarded as the management's monopoly. The prospect of making lower-level staff in effect collaborators in framing and actively implementing a set of ethics is one that many people in hierarchies will find hard to come to terms with, but it is a step that must be taken to respond appropriately to the pressures of the real-time world.

Beyond these organisational issues, real-time developments are having another effect the implications of which could turn out to be deeply damaging, to both principles of democracy and the ethical basis of many organisations. The expected effect of more widely available and faster communications may be more open and accountable decision-making, but there are signs that the opposite is likely to happen. As the document and decision-making trail becomes more accessible and discoverable, there is a good likelihood that really key decisions, ones whose discovery could harm the interests of the decision-makers and which are already made confidentially, will be pushed even more deeply underground, becoming more opaque and less disclosable than ever before.

This is a tendency embraced by illegal groups such as terrorists and organised criminals, but the prospect of being uncovered by a clever hacker or a satellite is likely to mean that legal state, non-state and private organisations are also more prone to make their most delicate decisions personally, face-to-face, with no electronic document trail to be exposed. This tendency, which is being exacerbated by the increasing preponderance of rules enforcing openness and disclosure of documents, is another paradoxical case of real-time technology leading to a step back from real-time practice, with significant ethical consequences.

As well as the changes in audience, organisations are under heavy pressure to shape a changed workforce to deal with the many and varied challenges of working in real time. As audiences and situations change rapidly, workforces need to be capable of slipping in and out of completely different modes of operation, each of which may be covered by differing ethical standards. The strongest example of this comes, once again, from the war in Iraq in 2003, when British troops found themselves in what has become known as the 'three-block war'. In three contiguous city blocks, the troops were engaged in three completely different kinds of operation. In one block they were conducting a frontal combat operation against organised units of the Iraqi Army, in the next they were engaged in operations against looters, and in the third their mission was to protect and care for refugees and to restore essential services. The three different situations required broadly different skills, sharply different operational standards and totally different ethical approaches towards the immediate audiences involved, while at the same time demanding a shared ethical base to the troops' conduct throughout. This was a clear, albeit extreme, example of the kind of operational and ethical flexibility needed by the workforces of many organisations in the real-time world.

The example of the 'ethical soldier' embodies the sort of varied decision-making that is becoming common to individuals in all kinds of organisations around the world in response to the pressures of the real-time world. Of course, having to make immediate decisions is not new. When, in the 1960s, US radar picked up something moving in the air from the Soviet Union, the US leadership had to decide in very real time whether the blob on the screen was an incoming nuclear attack or a flock of geese heading north for the summer. The difference today is that immediate decisions of that kind are no longer the preserve of senior military officers. At all levels in the military, the media, non-government organisations, development bodies and the financial markets, the real-time world means that snap decisions need to be made continuously, and decisions taken that way make the ethical base all the more important.

There are already countless examples of decisions being made too quickly or on the wrong ethical basis, or real-time actions being taken than have resulted in markets being tampered with, stocks being driven down by hoaxes, footage being broadcast that shouldn't have been and good reputations being demolished. The array of new challenges today alone, without even looking at the future, is phenomenal.

A 'prove it' world: ethical challenges of real time tomorrow

Looking ten years into the future, these ethical challenges are likely to intensify as real-time technology continues to develop and become even more ubiquitous. Perhaps the most important future challenge, one that will run through many of the others, is the increasing breakdown of trust – trust in organisations, trust between organisations and the individuals within them, trust in sources of information and trust in political and financial institutions.

For humanitarian organisations, the shift from a 'trust me' to a 'prove it' world triggered by real-time technology will cause a major transformation. The core element of the activity of organisations such as the ICRC is managing trust at the individual and global level, and if they have to prove themselves before they enter an area where aid is needed they will require a completely new method of working, and that means a new set of ethics. The trust these organisations have traditionally depended on has been built largely on discipline, on the ability of their delegates to portray the organisation in the necessary way by being neutral and efficient. Delegates are becoming increasingly challenging in response to the changes brought by real time, and managing trust with those delegates will be a very difficult issue for such bodies ten years from now.

The continuing growth of information sources and communication systems will also deepen the problem for humanitarian organisations of assessing the risks in a particular country, encumbered as they will be, like all of us swamped by real-time information, with the difficult question of deciding which version of reality is reliable or, to come back to the central issue, trustworthy. Another problem for them will be the probable further development of the system of international penal courts, which, when combined with real-time information, could make life very difficult for humanitarian operatives out in the field. Real-time information provided by those operatives could be used as evidence against local warlords and the like, blowing another hole in the trust upon which the ICRC and others depend. Any sensible warlord is likely to decide that having an ICRC representative in his country is therefore not worth the risk, and will refuse them access or worse.

One possible consequence of the explosion of information in real time could, paradoxically, be a revival of trust as a necessary component of forming ethics. It can be argued that we are heading for a ceiling of absorption, of technological development, beyond which people and organisations are incapable of absorbing any more. A situation of over-information would mean that the best route to finding a reliable source of reality would be by reverting to good old-fashioned trust. Swamped by endless sources and information, reverting to a trusted source for both information and ethical guidance could well be the only sane and workable solution. This is another example of the paradox that technology expected to solve problems on a rational basis will have led to a return to inter-subjectivity.

For news organisations in the next ten years the pressure of real time is likely to become an issue of survival. The fact that there are many more people now who can get into the business of information exchange – and there's no reason to believe that number won't continue to rise – raises questions about who the audiences are and who the originators are, whether they're telling the truth and why audiences would choose to believe one origi-nator and not another. Organisations such as the BBC hope that their reputation for impartial, accurate and reliable information will somehow maintain audiences' trust in these changing condi-tions, and they're preparing for it as best they can. Part of that preparation at the BBC is to make sure that everybody working there is provided with a firm understanding of the corporation's ethical framework and the importance of that framework. There's a constant struggle within the BBC to get programme-makers to understand that they have a responsibility beyond the programme they've made, that once the programme has gone to air it will have further implications for which they will be responsible. By taking this position, the BBC hopes that it will remain trusted as an ethically based provider of information.

Doers vs. watchers

Ten years from now another key feature is likely to be an ever-widening gap in many different senses between a minority that do and a majority that watch, due to developments in real-time technology. There will be those adept at handling and harnessing the new technological tools and making real time work for them and their organisations, and there will be a majority who simply watch the output from these forms of communication, are generally none the wiser for it and are slipping further from the doers in terms of social and political position, understanding and income. This fracturing is likely both within countries and in global terms.

For organisations, which are very often the source of a large slice of people's ethics, this will make it harder to recruit and retain the doers, and, as ever, the most effective way of keeping them will be by giving them more money. The political effects of a markedly increased polarisation of income and access to power and prestige could be catastrophic, and the ethical implications of having a small set of increasingly wealthy doers and a large set of increasingly impoverished watchers will be significant.

Another key ethical problem for organisations will be the probable deepening of the difficulty in maintaining reputations in an environment of increasing real-time information. The reputations of individuals, companies, institutions and governments will all be much more vulnerable, and organisations are going to need to work at and invest in reputation management. The expedient solution favoured today is often to drop an offending individual out of the boat for the good of the organisation's reputation. This will, however, sit uneasily with trying to build a relationship of trust between an organisation and its people, highlighting a point of ethical conflict between real-time, real-world processes on the one side and the quest for organisational stability on the other.

The quest to build trust in organisations is also likely to be complicated ten years from now by the increased expectations of stakeholders, due to their ability to keep a close and immediate eye on the activities of the organisation in real time. This is a trend already apparent in many areas, such as among humanitarian organisations, some of whose donors want to know what is being done with the specific parcel of money they have donated. Many such bodies already respond to their donors in this individualised way, and this approach is likely to continue and spread to other organisations as a way to entice their various stakeholders to remain connected, if not committed, to the organisation.

The political sphere is another area where the pressures caused by real time are likely to lead to the dissolution of trust. It's straightforward enough today to set up a political campaign with just a website, but the technology ten years from now is likely to have made real-time political campaigning even simpler. But what ethical criteria will be available to help people decide which campaigners to trust, which are genuine and which cranks? Whereas traditional political campaigns involve at some stage physically looking at the leaders and making a judgement, campaigns run through the Internet or mobile telephones, although they can mobilise millions to jam switchboards or swing opinion polls, usually don't even have to pass through this most basic filter.

The increasing availability of information in real time is likely to stimulate the growth of 'crowd pressure' to the point where it's a major factor in public life in ten years' time. As the technology develops, the crowd is likely to become larger and more dynamic, but the question remains about whether it will be any better informed. There's no guarantee that the information that gets crowd pressure going will be any more reliable than it is today, and as there is likely to be even less appetite for edited information, there can be no certainty about the basis upon which people will make their decisions about who and what to trust.

Real-time crowd pressure is already beginning to have a considerable impact. In the aftermath of 9/11, many chat rooms in the US were filled with virulent anti-Muslim material, and contributors egged each other on into virtual frenzies about killing all Muslims and burning down mosques. A decade from now there will be much greater potential for a real-time conflagration of this kind to develop very quickly, and the chances are that, as in the post-9/11 case, people will tend not to allow themselves to be challenged by information that is inconvenient to their prejudices, but will only go further in the direction in which they're already pointing.

Real action in real time: how to face the ethical challenge

What can be done to face the ethical challenges posed by the real-time world in ten years' time? The answer is a multi-faceted one involving individual personal responsibility, changes in organisational culture and a fundamental shift in the way legitimacy is constructed. It can be broadly set out in three main areas: how ethical standards are to be defined and by whom; the question of whose ethics are the right ones and where public responsibility lies; and how to find systemic ways of building a new ethical culture.

Defining the standards

The first point to be addressed when dealing with the definition of standards is whether there's a workable possibility of an international body that monitors ethics, sets standards and is regarded as having the authority to pronounce on the subject. The possible models are organisations such as the ICRC and Amnesty International, which in effect lay down standards of behaviour in the areas in which they are active that are generally regarded as the best in those areas, even by those who deliberately ignore them.

The other model is the United Nations. A nation intending to conduct a war of choice – rather than one of necessity – still needs at least to go into discussions with the UN beforehand, even if it ultimately ignores the UN's position, which indicates that the UN's standards are still widely accepted as the ideal ones. However, the problems of compliance which have beset the UN in recent years would be unlikely to be any less pronounced with a body aiming to set the standards on ethics. The appearance of the black helicopters of the ethics corps would be even less welcome in many quarters of the world than the blue helicopters of the UN.

An alternative, more generally palatable possibility is the

growth of several institutions, rather than one, which together could lay out ethical standards to meet the challenges of the real-time world, setting guidelines and pronouncing judgement on the relative ethical merit of different organisations and modes of behaviour. The models for these kinds of monitor are bodies such as the Poynter Institute in the US, which monitors standards in journalism. Encouraging equivalent bodies in different industries and areas of activity could result in the creation of a general ethical network providing a solid basis of values.

Leading operators in various fields that are already known for their ethics are another promising source of broader standard-setting. The trend in the 1990s towards the establishment of codes of conduct in different areas is unlikely to prove robust enough to deal with the ethical challenges posed by real time, but the rigorous development of a small number of organisations that not only articulate the highest standards but actively embody them in all their operations could provide a firm ethical basis.

As an example, the BBC currently fills this role among UK media organisations, and its management are well aware that its position as a standard-setter, besides being a strong part of its identity, will be an important component of its chances of survival in the fast-changing media world of the next ten years. They know that if the corporation is to continue to have a useful role, it has to find a way of translating its current 'trusted guide' status into activities that will maintain and strengthen that position. The BBC displays its editorial guidelines on its website, both as a way of making the public aware of its standards and as an instrument with which to encourage its staff how to think and behave, and it is strongly conscious of promoting and living those values in all its activities. In recent years, moves in this direction have been made by a number of news organisations, which have published for the first time statements of their standards and established publicised guidelines for their staff when dealing with issues such as conflicts of interest, largely in response to the need for transparency brought on by real-time technology.

Equivalent roles could easily be taken up, where they're not already, by humanitarian organisations, non-government bodies, state agencies and private-sector organisations, with one or two organisations in each sector building an explicit values base until they are perceived as the organisations that define standards.

From the military world, one mechanism for standard-setting that could be adapted more broadly is the concept of rules of engagement. These published rules, which specify which actions by a country's military forces are acceptable in which situations, are a fundamental tool of the military, and at their very base is concern for the other person, which is arguably at the centre of all ethics. The codification and publication of the equivalent of rules of engagement for all the organisations active in different fields could be hugely useful in finding out what is possible, building confidence among individual members of the organisation and articulating an ethical position, and could be used to push in the direction of an all-encompassing ethical framework.

One other possible source of standards in the future lies beyond the scope of organisations. As the problem of trust created by real-time developments undermines the position of larger institutions as sources of values, smaller clusters such as family, school friends and colleagues will become far more important in shaping standards.

Public responsibility

This last trend illustrates the central issue in the second broad area in responding to the ethical challenges of real time: the question of whose ethics should be taken up and the role of the public's responsibility. As traditional trust in institutions is eroded by real-time developments, the responsibility of the public as creators and implementers of their own ethics must expand to fill the gap. Hitherto, the world has been marked by constraint, in which we have all been constrained by the environment created on the basis of received ethical standards. As the changes in information, access and transparency continue in the next ten years, the world will be increasingly one of self-constraint, in which as consumers of information, producers of information, consumers more broadly and citizens, the burden of limitation on our actions will be our own. This is a geometrical shift in the ethical equation.

One notion that will be highly useful for creating ethics in a world marked by self-constraint is that of the common good. This is a fuzzy notion still in its infancy, but it is one that will be centrally important in a world where the public is responsible for its own ethical framework. Unlike the more limited concept of the common interest, the common good is not about the good of society as a general interest or the sum of the well-being of every individual in the society, but includes the dimensions of the good of the community itself and the good of all the members of the community. The question of how to arrive at and spread the notion of the common good is one well worth examining.

Neither self-constraint nor the concept of the common good can be imposed from above, and therefore awareness about norms and standards needs to be built among the public as a first step in establishing an ethical consensus, while putting pressure on institutions to act appropriately. The individual members of the crowd have personal responsibilities, and those responsibilities will be to a certain extent enhanced by some of the real-time technologies, which offer greater opportunities for participation and less excuse for passivity. Whatever ethical standards are coming down from institutions above, real-time technologies make many things possible from below, including malicious chat rooms, weblogs and similar phenomena, which can undermine the entire ethical structure. Whether as a consumer, a citizen or a weblogger, the individual has a responsibility not to behave like an idiot.

The signs are that the surfeit of information and bewildering array of information sources created in real time are already pushing many people towards overtly ethical viewpoints as a way of choosing what to rely on, rather than taking more rationalist approaches. The appeal of having somebody with a clearly stated ethical position telling you right from wrong in these conditions is seductive, which perhaps explains the growth of both Islam and fundamentalist Christianity, doctrines that can provide certainty in the increasingly uncertain world created by real-time technology. Leaving religion aside, however, there are signs of a growing concern for dealing with ethical questions that could be promising for the construction of a popularly rooted ethical framework over the next ten years.

Recent research by the BBC into the attitudes of young people and their parents towards the lyrics of popular songs threw up interesting results. While parents in general were concerned about descriptions of sex and violence, young people were disturbed by lyrics that showed signs of racism, sexism or homophobia. These results indicate that, while the ethical universe of young people may be different from that of their parents, it is no less rigorous. Similarly, research undertaken by the British Army in the 1990s showed that 60 per cent of people joining the army were doing so because, in part, they were explicitly seeking a community, one with a clear statement of its shared values.

The decline of political legitimacy has also made ethics far more important for many people than they were just a few decades ago. In the 1960s and 1970s politics was widely regarded as the way to solve global and social problems, whereas today politics in many countries is among the least respected of professions. The result is a trend best described by a leftist professor in Paris who said that thirty years ago when he wanted to engage students he talked about politics and when he wanted a light-hearted exchange he talked about ethics, but that today it's exactly the reverse. The demise of the legitimacy of politics and the uncertainties created by the real-time world are combining to create a strong and willing base for the establishment of sound ethical frameworks.

The systemic response

When it comes to the third main strand of building an ethical response to the real-time issues of the next decade – the systemic response – organisational initiative must by definition be central. To re-create the trust that is being undermined by real time, a new type of organisation will need to be created. Real-time developments mean that all kinds of stakeholders outside organisations will have far greater expectations that they used to and will be able to monitor the organisation's activities like never before. Maintaining trust will thus require an ability to respond more quickly and locally to their concerns, and that will mean constructing organisations in a far less centralised way than has traditionally been the case. To provide the flexibility needed to maintain the trust-based relationship between the organisation and its stakeholders, organisations may in effect need to build many different organisations within the one.

Within the organisation, maintaining the equally important trust-based relationship between the organisation and the individual – at a time when autonomy is more important than ever and one individual's action could destroy the organisation – will require an increased emphasis on ethical training, pulling as closely together as possible the individual's ethical sense and the organisational ethics. To do so will require building systems that encourage the individual not only to have a sense of responsibility but also to take responsibility.

Flowing from this, and linked to the current growth in ethical interest among young people, there's a possibility that organisations in ten years' time will be judged not so much on their impact or their financial results but on their values and the way they carry them out. It could well be that an organisation's fortunes, and its appeal to prospective recruits, will be determined largely by the sense of shared ethics it can offer its people and its stakeholders, how far those ethics correspond with those of the individual and how completely they are lived by the organisation.

Beyond the organisation, the growing importance of ethics formed by small local groups will create a new ethical landscape. With ethics in the real-time world being largely constructed, even to the point of deciding what is real and what is not, by small groups of family, friends and colleagues, the locus of ethical legitimacy will shift dramatically. Legitimacy will no longer be based upon institutional function but upon individual behaviour. If someone behaves in an ethically appealing manner, their view of reality and right and wrong is likely to be absorbed by others. Organisations, by creating a strong ethical base in which both individuals within the organisation and stakeholders are encouraged to participate, can have an indirect but seminal influence on this kind of ethical osmosis.

Thus, although the challenges to ethics caused by the arrival of the real-time world are clearly immense and are likely to become more pronounced over the next decade, there is plenty of scope for the development of an ethical framework to match them. There are institutions whose traditional strength as sources of ethics provides a good platform to begin a reshaping of the way standards and values are identified and applied. There is a growing recognition among those institutions and others that questions of ethics and trust will become questions of survival as the real-time world expands. And the uncertain world created by real-time technology, with its surfeit of information and plethora of sources, has triggered a strong and widespread hunger for ethical frameworks to help make sense of it all. However daunting the challenges, the clear and encouraging fact is that a real-time world does not have to be a world without ethics.

7

Conclusion:
Looking forward – what will change

Beth Krasna

Individuals are embedded in society and have external values, established by the group, and internal values, based around emotions and feelings. Value systems are incorporated into the biological basis of emotions and, although decisions are made rationally, there is a bodily state associated with the anticipation of the consequences of the decision. And this is influenced by free will. The notion of disconnection – where there is no link between the decision taken and its consequence – can be prevented by limiting the size of the group the individual is incorporated into. Helping people connect helps them to be ethical. If behaving ethically increases people's well-being, then they will naturally do what brings them pleasure. Individual consciousness and society's ethics will thus be incorporated into an individual's own value system.

Individuals who factor in all the facets of their lives – work, home, community – when they make decisions are more likely to behave ethically. This integration of roles will increase not only on the individual level but also in the knowledge sphere. The limits of specialisation in science are being reached and there is a need to reintegrate ethical considerations. Data is accumulating at an alarming rate, but it is value-free. As we move from information to knowledge and on to wisdom, we see an increasing ethical implication. The knowledge society is just at its beginning, and knowledge today is both specialised, fractal and unevenly distributed. The digital divide issue will be solved by technology within the next ten years, but this accumulation of knowledge is helping some parts of society more than others and the resulting schism will have to be addressed.

In ten years' time ethics will be a major factor in decision-making. There will be a need to harmonise ethics in order to avoid cross-contamination – between ethics and science, for example – and to ensure that science is working to find solutions to the major problems of humanity. Value creation will be measured by different criteria. Already we see trends in the private sector to include ethical, societal and environmental criteria next to financial measurements, and to see more accountability and performance measurements in the public sector. In a first phase we expect to see a proliferation of standards and rankings, which will raise awareness, followed by a consolidation of some of the standards. In any case, the trend towards increased transparency will continue, as will the costs of compliance and communication. Performance will be based more on future objectives than on the past, thus allowing for measurement of intent and achievement.

Rules, box-ticking and checklists will not be sufficient; there will be a need to create core values and embed them into an organisation. Brands and reputation will become more important, and the volatility around reputations will increase. With the decentralisation of decision-making and the empowerment of employees, individual integrity will become even more critical. Organisations will be investing in education and training, not so much on the rules but on the integration of ethical considerations in decision-making; the emphasis is moving from procedures to substance.

Reputation management will vastly increase in importance. Real-time technologies will enhance transparency and impact on decision-making, and can damage relationships between organisations and individuals. In order to maintain trust, there will be a need for organisations to show initiative in establishing standards. As audiences for these standards will be both internal and external, ethical practices will need to take them into account. Stakeholder issues will become more important, with trust as the main criterion. Some kind of policing, most probably self-policing, will become mainstream.

No international authority will be able to impose a compendium of standards; there would be too much resistance. There will be an increasing need to recognise not only diverse values but also the diverse sources of values. Responsibility will lie not only with the producers of the values but also with the recipients to participate in the debate, because they now have greater access to the information.

As people and organisations change only under pressure, we can expect to see more disobedience as a form of protest to bring about social change. Disobedience is a form of obedience to a higher moral order and, in its constructive form, can be considered a moral duty. Unfortunately, there will probably be an increase in violent disobedience as a means of protest against an unfair distribution of power, where too many majorities do not sufficiently protect the minority rights, and where there is a stalemate.

Individual integrity and moral courage are necessary to whistle-blow, as it is a challenge to group norms and can cause rejection, reprisals and punishment. In ten years' time, as we move towards more reputation management and self-policing, whistle-blowing will increasingly be considered a civic duty and the price paid by the individual should diminish. Constructive disobedience will be actively nurtured through dialogue and tolerance in the face of diversity; by speaking out and encouraging people to have the necessary moral courage to do so; and by educating the young on how to think rather than what to think.

In ten years' time we expect education (dispensed by schools, businesses and organisations) to focus on producing individuals with a strong identity and with an integrated perception of themselves in their different roles, thus allowing them to deal with increasing diversity. These people will consciously, and also unconsciously, behave more ethically.

Participants and contributing writers

Chapter 2: ETHICS AND CONSCIOUSNESS

Writer/rapporteur
Christine Wicker is an American journalist, previously with the *Dallas Morning News*, and author of *Not in Kansas Anymore: The Curious Tale of How Magic is Changing America*, to be published in October 2005, and *Lily Dale: The True Story of the Town that Talks to the Dead*.

Participants
Dieter Baumann is a Swiss lieutenant-colonel and battalion commander in the Swiss Army and a research assistant and teacher at the Swiss Military Academy at the Swiss Federal Institute of Technology in Zurich. He is doing a PhD in theology at Berne University.

Neville Hodgkinson, a British citizen, worked for thirty years as a journalist, including seven years as medical and science correspondent of the *Sunday Times*. He is the author of *Will to be Well – the Real Alternative Medicine* and *AIDS: The Failure of Contemporary Science*. He is, through the organisation Images and Voices of Hope, involved in an ongoing international debate about the role of the media. He is also part of the Brahma Kumaris World Spiritual University in Oxford.

Christian Kornevall, a Swedish citizen living in Zurich, is Senior Group Vice-President, Head of Sustainability Affairs, for the ABB Group. He is also Vice-Chairman of CSR Europe and the ABB Liaison Officer for the World Business Council for Sustainable Development. He was previously Deputy Director General at World Wildlife Fund International.

Dr Pierre J. Magistretti, a Swiss citizen and chairman of the workshop, is Professor of Psychiatric Neuroscience, Director of the Center for Psychiatric Neuroscience at the University of Lausanne Medical School and Professor at the Brain and Mind Institute at the Ecole Polytechnique Fédérale de Lausanne. Previously, he was the Vice-Dean of the University of Lausanne Medical School.

Michael Stopford, is Head of Global Public Affairs and Government Relations for Syngenta International. He was formerly with the ExxonMobil Corporation, following twenty years with the United Nations and the World Bank in New York,

Geneva and Washington. He was also an administrator at the American University, Washington. Now a US citizen, his first position was with the UK diplomatic service.

Dr Christoph Stückelberger, a Swiss citizen, is Director of the Institute for Theology and Ethics of the Federation of Swiss Protestant Churches in Berne and Professor of Ethics at the University of Basle. He is Chairman of the Ecumenical Church Loan Fund International, a member of the Swiss Ethics Committee on Non-Human Gene Technology, a member of the Consultative Commission for International Cooperation of the Swiss government and President of its sub-commission World Trade Organisation.

Benedikt Vonnegut, a Swiss citizen who lives in Zurich, is Secretary of the Executive Committee of Holcim Ltd. He has worked extensively on formulating sustainable development policies for Holcim and the cement industry in general through Holcim's affiliation with the World Business Council for Sustainable Development.

Chapter 3: ETHICS AND KNOWLEDGE

Writer/rapporteur
Tim Hindle is a senior editor at *The Economist*, based in London. He writes about a wide range of subjects, mostly in the business and finance areas. He has also launched a number of magazines in different fields and he is the author of a pile of books, some in his own name, some in other people's. He lives in rolling English countryside with his Turkish wife.

Participants
William Davies, a British citizen, is a Senior Research Fellow at the Institute for Public Policy Research in London. He was previously a researcher at the Work Foundation. His research focuses on social uses of the Internet, social capital, wired communities, the digital divide and theories of the information society.

Dr Francis Gurry, an Australian, is the Deputy Director General of the World Intellectual Property Organisation (WIPO) in Geneva, where he is responsible for patents, traditional knowledge, genetic resources and the Arbitration and Mediation Center. Before joining WIPO, he practised as an attorney in Melbourne and Sydney and taught law at the University of Melbourne.

Dr Domènec Melé is Professor and Head of the Department of Business Ethics at the IESE Business School, University of Navarra, Spain. Previously he was Professor of Chemical Technology at the Polytechnic University of Valencia. Besides business ethics, his areas of interest are CSR, Christian ethics and spirituality in management, organisational culture, philosophy of management and corporate values. He has authored or edited fifteen books and more than fifty scientific articles.

Helen Sayers, who is from Jersey, coordinates Living Values Education in Switzerland. She is currently facilitating a project to implement living values in countries in sub-Saharan Africa, in partnership with UNESCO's regional Office for Education in Africa. She also represents the Brahma Kumaris World Spiritual University at the UN.

Dr Jean-Louis Vanherweghem, a Belgian, is President of the Université Libre de Bruxelles, a former rector and a full professor. He is also the head of the Department of Nephrology at the Erasme Hospital in Brussels. He is a member of several boards and of the Fonds National de Recherche Scientifique (Belgium) and a member of the Royal Academy of Medicine (Belgium).

Dr Francis Waldvogel, a Swiss citizen and the chairman of the workshop, is Honorary Professor of the Medical Faculty of Geneva University and a past president of the Swiss Federal Institutes of Technology. He was chairman of the Department of Medicine, Geneva University Hospital, and a professor in the departments of Internal Medicine and of Microbiology at the Geneva University Medical School.

Chapter 4: ETHICS AND PERFORMANCE

Writer/rapporteur
Garrick Holmes is an American business journalist with a special interest in the role of multinational corporations in economic globalisation. He is currently a contributing editor to two publications of the Economist Group, the newsletter *Business Europe* and the quarterly journal *European Policy Analyst.*

Participants
Dr Dominique Biedermann, a Swiss citizen, is the Executive Director of the Ethos Swiss Investment Foundation for Sustainable Development in Geneva. Prior to launching Ethos, he was Executive Director of the Canton of Geneva Pension Fund. He is also a member of the National Commission Justitia & Pax of the Swiss Roman Catholic Bishop Conference, and of the editorial committee of the Swiss pension funds' review *Schweizer Personalvorsorge.*

Matt Christensen, chairman of the workshop and a dual UK/US citizen, is the Executive Director of the European Social Investment Forum (Eurosif) in Paris. His prior positions were as strategy consultant with Braxton Associates and as European development director for the UK-based Motley Fool.

Dr Heidi Diggelmann is Honorary Professor at the Medical Faculty of the University of Lausanne. She was previously a leading Swiss scientist at the Swiss Institute for Experimental Cancer Research; a professor and the director of the Microbiology Institute at the University of Lausanne; and a past president of the Research Council of the Swiss National Science Foundation. Throughout her whole career she has been involved in issues of bio-safety and the relationship between science and society.

Pâquerette Girard Zappelli, a French citizen, is the International Olympic Committee Ethics Commission Special Representative, based in Lausanne. Prior to joining the IOC, she was a French judge and worked for the French Minister of Justice in the International Affairs Directorate, and at the Cour de Cassation in Paris.

Dr Robin Hodess, a US citizen, is Director of Policy and Research at the anti-corruption NGO Transparency International in Berlin. She was previously a programme officer working on issues of justice in the world economy with the Carnegie Council on Ethics and International Affairs in New York. Prior to this she taught media and politics at the Free University of Berlin and Leipzig University, focusing on the role of communication in political life.

Raphael Jaquet is a Swiss citizen and Vice-Chairman of the Board of Directors of KPMG Switzerland, the senior partner of the Geneva office and a member of the Audit Committee Institute founded by KPMG. He is a chartered accountant and licensed banking auditor recognised by the Swiss Federal Banking Commission. Prior to joining KPMG he was head of administration and chief accounting officer of a Geneva-based finance company.

Chapter 5: ETHICS AND DISOBEDIENCE

Writer/rapporteur
Fiona Fleck is a British, Geneva-based journalist who writes for the *New York Times* and many other publications on a wide range of subjects, from public health to private banking.

Participants

David Atwood, a US citizen who has lived in Europe for the past 27 years, is the Director of the Quaker United Nations Office and its Representative for Disarmament and Peace in Geneva. He is the former General Secretary of the International Fellowship of Reconciliation.

Steve Bowbrick, a British citizen, is the founder and CEO of Thinner Media, UK. He has ten years' experience in running Internet businesses and describes himself as an entrepreneurial manager with enthusiasm for technology, media and marketing.

Anton Hügli, a Swiss citizen, is Professor of Philosophy and Pedagogy at the University of Basle. His research focuses on the relationship between philosophy and pedagogy, and on the position of ethics in education. Among other books, he is the author of *Umweltbildung im 20. Jahrhundert* and *Kritik der Evaluation an Schulen und Hochschulen*.

William McComish, an Irishman, is Dean of Saint Pierre Cathedral in Geneva; General Treasurer of the World Alliance of Reformed Churches; and a former vice-president of the Geneva Protestant Church. He was also the chaplain at Armagh Prison in Northern Ireland. He is a member of the Davos Forum and his latest book is *Permettez-moi de m'expliquer.*

Dr Imam Abduljalil Sajid, chairman of the workshop, is a leading British Muslim of Pakistani origin who is Imam of the Brighton Islamic Mission. He also serves as Chairman of the Muslim Council for Religious and Racial Harmony, UK; Vice-Chair of the UK Chapter of the World Conference of Religions for Peace; and International Secretary of the World Congress of Faiths. Among other books, he has edited *Why Terror – Is There No Alternative? 19 Muslims Speak Out.*

Chapter 6: ETHICS IN REAL TIME

Writer/rapporteur

Richard Brass is an Australian freelance journalist based in London. A regular contributor to *The Times* and *Daily Telegraph*, he writes for a wide variety of publications on subjects ranging from business innovation to Rugby League to British pub culture. He is a former editor of *Punch* magazine.

Participants

Bebiana de Almeida, an Angolan citizen, is a Visiting Professor of International

Relations, University of Agostinho Neto in Luanda, Angola, and a consultant to several African governments on the subject of international cooperation and sustainable local development. She was formerly the coordinator of all the UN agencies and the resident representative of the United Nations Development Programme in the Republic of Central Africa.

Yves Daccord, a Swiss citizen, is the Director of Communications of the International Committee of the Red Cross in Geneva. Previously head of the Division for the Promotion of International Humanitarian Law, he has worked in Israel, Sudan, Yemen, the northern Caucasus and Georgia. He was formerly a journalist.

Dr Paul Dembinski, a Swiss citizen, is Professor of Economics at the University of Fribourg; Director of the foundation Observatoire de la Finance in Geneva; and co-founder of Eco'Diagnostic, also in Geneva. He is the editor of the bilingual publication *Finance & Bien Commun/Common Good.*

Major-General Sebastian Roberts, a British citizen, is currently commanding the British Army's London District. He is the former head of Corporate Communications of the British Army and was previously with their Doctrine Directorate, where he was involved in writing their ethical guidelines.

Dr Philip Seib, an American citizen, is chairman of the workshop. He is the Lucius W. Nieman Professor of Journalism at Marquette University, Milwaukee, and also the Director of the Nieman Symposia. His focus is media ethics, new technologies and international news coverage. He is the author of fourteen books, including *Going Live* and *Beyond the Front Lines*.

Stephen Whittle, a British citizen, is the Controller, Editorial Policy, at the BBC in London. He is also a member of the Parliamentary and Legal Committee of the Society of Editors. His previous job was Director of the Broadcasting Standards Commission. Prior to joining the BBC, he was the Deputy Director of Communication of the World Council of Churches in Geneva.